WHATEVER HAPPENED TO
EVANGELISM?

WHATEVER HAPPENED TO EVANGELISM?

A CALL FOR A RETURN TO BIBLICAL EVANGELISM

BY DANNY PELFREY

Foreword by
Dr. John Caldwell

CrossLink Publishing

CrossLink Publishing
1601 Mt. Rushmore Rd, STE 3288
Rapid City, SD 57702

Ordering Information:
Quantity sales. Special discounts are available on quantity purchases by corporations, associations, and others. For details, contact the "Special Sales Department" at the address above.

Whatever Happened to Evangelism?/Pelfrey —1st ed.

ISBN 978-1-63357-216-4

Library of Congress Control Number: 2019955151

First edition: 10 9 8 7 6 5 4 3 2 1

To Brian Smith, Gil Whitten, and Earl Lambert

Men with passion for souls

Contents

FOREWORD 3

CHAPTER 1: A PASSIONATE PLEA 5

CHAPTER 2: EVANGELISM AND THE HUMAN HEART 13

CHAPTER 3: EVANGELISM AND CHURCH LEADERSHIP .. 23

CHAPTER 4: EVANGELISM AND BASIC THEOLOGY 31

CHAPTER 5: SOME MISCONCEPTIONS ABOUT
EVANGELISM 39

CHAPTER 6: SEVEN SIGNIFICANT THOUGHTS FOR
EFFECTIVE EVANGELISM.. 47

CHAPTER 7: SEVEN MORE SIGNIFICANT THOUGHTS FOR
EFFECTIVE EVANGELISM.. 57

PART TWO: A PRACTICAL MANUAL FOR RETURNING TO
NEW TESTAMENT EVANGELISM 67

CHAPTER 8: HOW TO TELL YOUR STORY IN THREE
MINUTES 69

CHAPTER 9: A PRESENTATION FOR LEADING ONE TO
JESUS 77

CHAPTER 10: WHEN THE ANSWSER IS "NO" 87

CHAPTER 11: WHERE TO FIND THEM 97

CHAPTER 12: OLD IDEAS WITH POTENTIAL 105

CHAPTER 13: SCRIPTURE, QUOTATIONS, AND A FINAL WORD...115

FOREWORD

Dr. John Caldwell
Retired Pastor
Thirty-six years with Kingsway Christian Church
Avon, Indiana

D anny Pelfrey has not only been faithful to his Lord but has done the Church a real service in addressing the question, "Whatever Happened to Evangelism?" In a day and age where there is more "positive thinking preaching" in many pulpits than gospel preaching; where spectators often come to be entertained rather than convicted and challenged; it is time for the Church to get back to the basics. And nothing is more basic than reaching the lost. After all, that's why Christ came: *"For the Son of Man came to seek and save those who are lost"* (Luke 19:10). *"God sent his Son into the world not to judge the world but to save the world through him"* (John 3:17).

Ironically, just days before Danny sent me his manuscript, I had asked the very same question in my journal: "Whatever happened to evangelism?" I've been troubled by a lack of emphasis in the church on heaven, hell, sin, and salvation. We've become so politically correct that terms like "being saved," "soul-winning," and "born again" have all but disappeared from the Church's vocabulary. A majority of churches no longer have a public invitation in their services for people to come to Christ. Are you aware of any congregations that have regularly scheduled nights for evangelistic calling? In the church I served for 36 years, we did so every week for 36 years and with great results. By the way, no one could be an elder or staff member who did not himself regularly participate and share his or her faith.

The thing I appreciate about Danny's book is that he begins with the scriptural and philosophical basis for evangelism, but then gives practicum on how best to evangelize. Furthermore, he writes not theoretically but out of personal experience; and it is obvious that he knows whereof he writes.

I must admit that this book brought conviction to my heart as I realized that in retirement, I haven't really worked to expand my circle of unsaved friends and neighbors. I'm working on changing that. What about you? Is there someone with whom you know you should have shared your faith, but have failed to do so, perhaps out of fear of rejection? And what about your church? Is there a clearly defined strategy for reaching your community for Christ? My hope is that this book will be a turning point in the lives of many of us personally and the churches from which we come, as we recapture a zeal for reaching the lost.

CHAPTER 1

A PASSIONATE PLEA

It's been almost thirty years, but the events of the evening are still etched firmly in my mind. It was Tuesday night. Three out of every four Tuesday nights, twenty-five well-trained outreach workers from Town and Country Christian Church in Shelbyville, Indiana were turned loose on a five-county area. I was their minister. Brian, my visitation partner, and I had traveled across the Johnson County line for our second visit of the evening. The distance we traveled made us a little late getting back to home base. The trip home was enjoyable for me. I had opportunity to chat with Brian. He liked my southern twang, and I loved his British accent. The beautiful fall evening highlighted the stars shining brightly overhead. It was harvest time in Indiana. The farmers, not wanting to miss the opportunity the weather provided were out in full force. We could see the lights of their combines moving across the soybean and corn fields. A little earlier, it had occurred to me how symbolic it all seemed. The farmers were in the fields harvesting their crops while we were out, attempting to harvest souls.

As we approached the church building, my heart perhaps skipped a beat or two as my excitement level rose. "Look," I called out to Brian, "the lights are on in the auditorium." We both knew what that meant. The baptistry was in the auditorium. We were a church that often followed the book of Acts' example of baptizing the same hour. (See the accounts of the Ethiopian eunuch in Acts 8:26-40 and the Philippian jailer in Acts 16-29-33.) Lights on in the auditorium on a Tuesday evening almost always meant that someone had decided to accept the Lord, desiring to be baptized immediately. Brian and I hurried into the building where we joined several members of the visitation team sitting in pews near the front of the large assembly room. After a few moments, Steve, one of our visitation people, ushered a tall, dark-headed gentleman into the baptistry. I knew him to be a likable, successful businessman who recently had started attending our services. Steve put one hand on the small of the tall man's back while taking one of the man's wrist with his other hand. Looking into his eyes, he asked, "Do you believe that Jesus is the Christ, the Son of the Living God?" To which the candidate answered, "I do." With that answer Steve stated, "I baptize you in the name of the Father, the Son and the Holy Spirit." Steve lowered him into the water, then quickly helped him to his feet. It wasn't perfect form like I had been taught, but who cared? There was applause and a couple of "amens" from the observers who remained until their new brother came from the dressing room. Prayer followed and then handshakes and hugs. By the time I got home I was too excited to sleep. I had a new brother, and nothing is more thrilling than that. It is a scene that was played out time and time again in that Indiana church which obviously had learned what it meant to be The Church.

It was while I served that same congregation that I showed up at Bobby and Darlene's front door one evening. This couple along with their two young children had started attending our services regularly. Even though I had made no appointment, they readily welcomed me and seemed genuinely glad I was there. I had not intended to talk with them about their relationship with the Lord that evening, but they were so receptive that I decided I would throw caution to the wind. I proceeded by asking if I could share a few verses from the Bible with them. They immediately agreed. "We were hoping you would come by, but there's one thing. Could I go across the yard and get David and Shannon?"

Darlene asked. David and Shannon were a neighbor couple who had attended worship with them a couple of times. Darlene did bring them over. I shared with all four who agreed they were ready to accept the Lord. The two couples met me at the church building less than an hour later, and we had another of those unforgettable Philippian jailer moments.

A couple of years ago, my wife and I traveled from Georgia back to Shelbyville, Indiana to sign one of our inspirational mysteries at the Three Sisters Bookstore. It was great to be there after being away for a good number of years. We were thrilled that people had not forgotten us. There was a steady stream of friends for the entire three hours we were scheduled. They often sat down, and we talked of old times. Frequently, it was stories of people coming to know the Lord that they recalled. Later, when I had time to look back on that gathering, I realized that well over half those who dropped by to share were people who had come to know the Lord as a result of the Tuesday evening program.

"It was a magical time," one gentleman, now near his eighty-fifth birthday remarked, regarding those earlier years when evangelism was the focus at Town and Country. I don't know that I would use the word *magical,* but I would agree with him that it was a special time in my life. It was a time when I received my grandest satisfaction. It was a time when I felt most centered on the Lord's will. It was a time when evangelism was the passion of my life. *Lord, may it be true again!*

In the past, when one went into a Christian bookstore searching for help in developing his evangelistic skills, he might find shelves of books on the subject. Not any more or, maybe I'm going to the wrong stores. In those days there was always a *share your faith* seminar to attend if one was interested, but the mailings announcing such events seem to have ceased a while back. But maybe I'm no longer on their mailing lists. I used to hear people talking about the need to win souls. I miss that conversation. But my greatest concern is I don't see it happening much anymore. I recently found myself asking the question, whatever happened to evangelism? Maybe it's being done a different way under other headings, and I am ignorant of some wonderful results. After all, I'm not in the center of Christian activity like I once was. Regardless of what we call it, evangelism desperately needs to be in the forefront of a disciple's life, and at the center of the Church's work. When evangelism is ignored or neglected, souls are lost, the church is weakened, the Lord is let down, and great joy is forfeited. The neglect of evangelism by Christians may be among the worst tragedies of our age.

When I decided to give this little volume its title, I thought long and hard before dubbing it *Whatever Happened to Evangelism?* I was worried that such a title would cause potential readers to be turned off, thinking it is a negative work. I thought that title might suggest the author is like the preacher who is ready to point out the problem without serving up a solution. I certainly didn't want to do that. It is true that much will be made of the problem. In any situation, a remedy cannot be found until the problem is fully diagnosed. So, we are going to dive into the problem as I see it. But we will also look diligently for solutions. I decided to stay with the title because I want it to be a call to wake-up and refocus on this all-important matter of evangelism.

It appears that church people are always looking for that innovation - that new way of getting it done whatever *it* might be. Maybe the key is in the latest book or perhaps it will be the subject of the most recent seminar to which we are invited. "Got to be an easier way to get it done," we groan. I have concluded regarding evangelism that we would do well to look *back* to find the best way to go forward. Maybe we need to refocus on the past. That does not mean that changes in our culture should not be considered. But it does mean we need to start in the first century and make our way from there. Maybe it's the old that we need to be searching out instead of the new.

How important is evangelism to the church and to the individual disciples of Jesus? Let's go back two thousand plus years and revisit a scene on a Galilean hillside to find an answer to that question. When Jesus's disciples followed his instructions and met Him there, mixed emotions were in evidence. We are told they worshipped Him, but some doubted. I think most of them realized by then that Jesus was about to leave them. When he started to talk, they were, no doubt, locked onto his words. He was about to give them their final instructions. His message is recorded in Matthew 28:18-20. The resurrected Christ reminded them, "All authority in heaven and on earth has been given to me." He was telling them there were no options as to whether or not his instructions would be obeyed. His Father, the God of Heaven, had granted him all authority. It was his way of saying, *You fellows had better listen up. This is important!*

Jesus went on from there to layout their assignment. "Therefore, go and make disciples of all nations..." According to none other than Jesus Himself, the disciple's commission is to go and make disciples for Him. However, He did not leave it there. He told them there were two factors necessary to accomplish such a task. "Baptizing them in the name of the Father and of the Son and of the Holy Spirit." That is evangelism, the leading of a person to commit his life to Jesus. He is saying that bringing one to a state of discipleship demands first the conversion of that individual. But Jesus knew that disciple-making had to go a step beyond that. He continued, "...teaching them to obey everything I have commanded you." After one is converted to Jesus he must be taught and encouraged to follow the Word of God. So, the second step to making disciples is to add to the convert's spiritual strength by teaching him/her all of God's Word. We may refer to this as edification or a half dozen other terms, but the fact is Jesus was careful to point out to his disciples that the job of disciple-making does not end in the baptistry.

At that moment, the disciples must have been thinking, *He's expecting a lot of us. How could we possibly accomplish such a difficult task without Him here to lead us?* But Jesus anticipated that concern. He assured them with fourteen beautiful words, "...and surely I am with you always, to the very end of the age." It took me a long time to get a firm hold on that important fact. There is nothing that Jesus wants me to do that I cannot do. That is true not because of my great strength and ability. I decided long ago that I am no more than an average mortal at best. I can do whatever Jesus wants me to do because He will provide the strength and the ability that I am lacking for that task. We can be successful not because we are special, but because He is great.

Let's do a quick review of that mountain moment where Jesus commissioned his disciples for all generations. He clearly explained that the disciple's mission is to make other disciples. That is our primary purpose as his disciples. How do we do it? First, we bring people to Jesus. The second step is to build them up in the Lord through the Word. Jesus assured us that we can do the job because He is with us. It's a simple formula for saturating the world with a core of devoted followers. Yet, it seems to me that with each generation, the Church is straying further and further away from the plan.

Many church leaders would agree that this is the way to success for the Church. They might even agree with me that church programs should be evaluated by their effectiveness in accomplishing at least one of the two stated steps for making disciples. But here is the problem that caused me to feel this book and others like it are necessary for twenty-first century Christians. Most of those church leaders who claim to believe in the validity of the Great Commission would declare that their calling is to provide muscle for the second step for making disciples. *God has called us to be a teaching church. It is ours to edify. God calls others to evangelize.* We will address the why of such a conclusion later. Oh, they believe some evangelism will happen along the way, but as far as they are concerned, that is the task assigned to someone else. The problem with that is it throws the whole process off balance. People can only be built-up in the Lord after they are won to the Lord. It is not hard to see what happens if almost everyone is edifying and practically no one is evangelizing. It is not a question of one step being more important than the other. It is a question of proper order. One must be won before he can be built-up in the Lord. For the Lord's discipleship program to work, reaching must take priority because one cannot grow in the Lord until he is first won to the Lord. It starts with evangelism!

FOR YOUR CONSIDERATION

1. Is it practical to follow the example of "same-hour baptism" found in Acts 8:26 and 16:29-33?

2. Do you know anyone who has been won to the Lord through a church visitation program?

3. Can a church evangelistic calling program work in our day?

4. Is the author correct in assuming that today Christians are giving less attention to evangelism than in times past?

5. What caused you to come to that conclusion?

6. Is the title of this book, Whatever Happened to Evangelism? an appropriate title?

7. What did Jesus state as the primary task of his disciples?

8. What are the two steps to attaining the goal Jesus set for us?

9. Is one step more important than the other?

10. In one sentence, why is it possible for us to successfully do the task to which Christ called us?

CHAPTER 2

EVANGELISM AND THE HUMAN HEART

I was told of the comic script character who was pictured with a sword made of sticks raised high. The words inscribed in the balloon drawn over his head declared, "We have met the enemy, and he is us!" We can be our own worst enemy when it comes to our involvement in biblical evangelism. Whether we follow the Lord's plan to involve ourselves in the first step to making disciples is our choice. Will we choose to be obedient to the Lord or will we choose to ignore his final instructions?

Many would excuse themselves from involvement on the basis that they are not qualified. "I don't have the gift of evangelism," they would argue. Let me clearly state that it is obvious to me there are Christians who have been endowed with the gift of evangelism. Those are the people we hear about who whip out their New Testament on the plane and lead the passenger seated next to them to the Lord before they land. They are the people who dare go "soul-winning" at midnight on the streets of New York City. I am not one of those people. I wish I were, but I'm not.

The Lord has honored me by allowing me to lead hundreds of souls to Him, but I do not possess the gift of evangelism. I will explain later in this chapter why I know that is true. But what we need to know is that we read nowhere in God's word where evangelism is to be left only to those who have a gift for it. When

I read God's Word, I see a call to Christians in general to participate in this important work of the kingdom. It is a *disciple thing.* It is not the gifted evangelist who will get us back on track, but those who are willing to step outside their comfort zones to perform that important task. The work may come extremely hard for them, but they are the key.

Then, why are some given the gift of evangelism and others are not? I don't know the answer to that question. The Lord didn't choose to tell us, and I can't read his mind. The Lord's intentions for us seem to be clear when we read such passages as Luke 10:2 where Jesus instructed, "... The harvest is plentiful, but the workers are few. Ask the Lord of the harvest, therefore, to send out workers into the harvest field." So many of the Lord's parables such as *The Lost Sheep, The Lost Coin, and The Lost Boy* (Luke 15:1-32) deal either directly or indirectly with the subject of evangelism. Then there is The Great Commission which we discussed in the previous chapter. It would appear to me that for us to try to opt out for whatever reason may be nothing more than rationalization.

Long ago when I was a freshman student at little Atlanta Christian College (now Point University), I had a one-hour-a-week class in *personal evangelism.* In one of those classes, Reggie Thomas, the instructor, told us the story of a lady who had seen many birthdays. She was struggling with several debilitating health issues. Despite that, she was able to make it to church one Lord's day, though in some pain. It happened to be a day when the preacher came down hard on his congregation about the need to share Christ. "All of us must share Christ," He told them. The elderly lady was convicted but torn. On the way out of the building she said to her preacher, "You don't mean me. Why, I can't do that! I'm confined to my home. Only occasionally am I able to go outside those doors. How could I possibly share Christ with anyone? Surely, you don't mean me."

"Yes, even you," the preacher insisted. "Are there people who come to your home?" he asked.

"Yes, she answered after a brief deliberation. "There are some delivery people and medical workers who are occasionally there."

"Do they all know the Lord?" the preacher asked her.

"I don't know," she admitted.

"Maybe those are your opportunities," he suggested.

Throughout the first part of that week, the lady pondered her preacher's remarks. Then on Thursday the dry-cleaning man showed up to deliver items she had allowed him to take when he was there a week earlier. As he was leaving, she nervously blurted out, "Sir, do you know Jesus as your personal Savior?"

The man stood for a few silent moments looking into her eyes before the tears began to flow. Finally, he answered, "No ma'am, I don't. It's been on my mind for a while now. Could you tell me how I can receive Him?" According to Mr. Thomas, that lady led her visitor to the Lord that day. By the end of the year, several more people who regularly came to her home had also been reached. Much can be accomplished when we yield to our hearts and simply respond to the Lord's call.

Let's consider some of the internal obstacles that tend to stifle the work of evangelism to which we have been called.

FEAR!

Fear is one of Satan's most tattered tools, for he uses it regularly. It has been my observation that fear is often the factor that causes the Lord's work to be left undone. How can fear be an obstacle to evangelism?

The fear that comes with natural or unnatural timidity can stifle one's desire to evangelize. Even some of the most extroverted people I have known tell me they are shy, and they probably are. My research revealed that about fifty percent of people are probably introverted, while the other fifty percent tend to be extroverted. What does that mean? That simply means that for half of us, our energy comes from within, and the other half are energized by direct interaction with people. Shyness is a fear or anxiety about social situations or contact with other individuals. Both introverts and extroverts can experience shyness. Studies reveal that the introvert is probably only slightly more susceptible to true shyness than the extrovert. Six to seven percent of people likely suffer from a more extreme social disorder that causes them to avoid people because of their fear of being humiliated, judged, and rejected. Probably, only the most extroverted (maybe the top five percent or so) along with the few that seem to have the gift of evangelism would be totally at ease with doing evangelism. So, who do those stats excuse from the work of evangelism? My answer? Nobody!

Almost everyone who has known me well will tell you I have spent my life struggling with timidity, perhaps being among the six or seven percent most affected. Yet, those same people would, most likely, affirm that personal evangelism has been my most visible contribution to the Lord's kingdom. In middle school, a teacher gave me the nickname, The Sphinx. In me, Jack Purcell saw a silent stone-face boy, uncomfortable around almost all people. Not a good recommendation for one who would someday knock on doors to talk with people about Jesus. But I knew I didn't have a choice when as a young adult I became acutely aware of the Lord's commission. I would have to bite the bullet, step well outside my comfort zone, and give it my best effort. There were times when it took every ounce of determination I could muster to convince myself to knock on that door. Many times, I knocked while praying no one was home. Sometimes it was a pathetic stutter-filled presentation that followed, leaving me rather discouraged with a lot of doubts. Mostly people rejected those pleas to accept Christ, but sometimes they gave their lives to the Lord. It took awhile, but the time came when most of my fear was gone. Of all my duties, I came to look forward most to those times of speaking with people about Jesus. Eventually, I came to realize I did not have to be afraid. I found myself one day actually declaring, "This is fun!"

Here are three simple steps we can take to allow us to overcome the fear that might otherwise fill our hearts and repress the desire to evangelize. *First, we must apply ourselves to grow our faith in Jesus.* Remember Jesus's last words before leaving this world? We discussed them in the previous chapter: "And surely I am with you always, to the very end of the age" (Matthew 28:20). We are most comfortable in doing evangelism when we truly believe that. Elizabeth Elliot reminded us, "Fear arises when we imagine that everything depends on us." Looking to Jesus enables us to find needed help. No reason to be fearful. Everything doesn't depend on us. It's really a matter of trusting the Lord's strength, ability, and love. We call that faith.

Secondly, prepare well. In those early days, I found a lot of courage when I put together a presentation for use in leading people to the Lord. I wrote it out and memorized it. Then I placed an empty chair in front of me. For several weeks, I sat down and converted that empty chair regularly until I could recite my presentation without any hesitation whatsoever. From time to time, I have polished my little speech a bit but have continued to use the basic concept for decades. Because of its no frills style, I was surprised when I was frequently asked to teach it to people throughout the Midwest. Having such a presentation firmly planted in my mind helped to alleviate fear from my heart. Knowing what I would say and how I would say it took away much of the anxiety, gave me confidence I otherwise would not have had.

The third step in overcoming the fear of evangelism is to keep on keeping on. The more we do a thing, the more at ease we are with it. It didn't happen overnight; but ultimately, I became almost perfectly at ease with talking to people about their relationship with Jesus. That never would have happened if evangelism had not become a regular part of my life.

Will all the fear that comes with the practice of what we call evangelism ever be eliminated? Probably not for most of us. A heart of courage is a key. Remember that courage is not the absence of fear, but it is the mastery of fear, the ability to go on even in the face of fear. I am often drawn to David's words in Psalm 27:3: "Though an army besiege me, my heart will not fear; though war break out against me, even then I will be confident."

SLOTH!

Sloth is an inward condition, a condition of the heart, that leads to reluctance to exert one's self. Sometimes it is used as a synonym for laziness, but I would rather think of sloth as the condition and laziness as the result. Regardless of the particularities of the definition, the fact is it can be a major obstacle to the work of evangelism. The writer of Proverbs 26:15 gave us a hint to the type of problem we are here addressing when he wrote, "A sluggard buries his hand in the dish; he is too lazy to bring it back to his mouth."

We are told in Ecclesiastes 10:18, "Through laziness, the rafters sag; because of idle hands, the house leaks." The point is that laziness often prevents the completion of important work. Such a heart condition is certainly an enemy to the Lord's work and to the act of evangelism in particular.

Sloth can take on several forms as it relates to the Lord's call to evangelism. *First, there is the person who has little motivation for any hard work of any kind.* In my youth, I heard an older gentleman, himself one of the most motivated men I ever knew, say of an acquaintance, "He couldn't hold a job as a taster in a pie factory." Not a nice thing to say of anyone, but it is true there are people in this world who fall into that classification. They are not willing to exert any real energy on any project. We are not talking about people who can't but people who won't. It's going to be difficult to get any work out of them until the Lord brings about some significant changes in their hearts.

Secondly there are those who will substitute less strenuous activity for that which is for them difficult labor. Someone remarked, "the most serious idleness of all is being busy with things that matter very little." People who find evangelism hard will sometimes trade it off for something they find to be less difficult. I have often felt that even vocational church leaders can be guilty. They will give the bulk of their time to fighting over church doctrines, traditions, social issues, building programs, or some other concerns. This may help them, in their own hearts to justify their neglect. Understand that I am not suggesting there are no other worthwhile tasks to be performed, but as disciples who have been commissioned by Jesus, evangelism should be included. It should be given a place of priority.

Then there are those who will tell you they are waiting on a more convenient time - the procrastinators. I cannot recall the author who wrote the statement I read recently, "A lazy person speaks much about yesterday and tomorrow." One may think he can hide his laziness by talking about what he did in the past and what he intends to do in the future. The Lord is most interested in what we are doing *now*. While we are waiting for tomorrow or looking back at yesterday, opportunity may be passing us by.

The one with a heart of sloth may find it necessary to offer a lot of excuses for lack of participation in jobs like evangelism which they find exhausting. Proverbs 22:13 is rather humorous. I guess it's one of those statements that would be funny if not so bitterly true. The writer says, "The sluggard says, 'There's a lion outside! I'll be killed in the public square." Do you understand what he is saying? He is suggesting that the sluggard or lazy man will make excuses like the possibility of being killed by a lion or being murdered if he leaves the house to go to work. That's reaching for an excuse, isn't it? Some of the excuses we offer and hear can be rather ridiculous. Some of them may sound pretty good. And some may not be excuses at all. They may be valid. Understand that I am not suggesting that everyone who does not participate in evangelism is a lazy sluggard. There are circumstances that can limit a person. However, even with difficult situations such as the lady we talked about in the beginning of the chapter who led her drycleaner to the Lord, one can often find a way.

It seems to me the disciples of the first century turned the world upside-down because their hearts had been turned right-side up. That is the only answer to transforming the slothful Christian. We will never strong-arm him or her into serving the Lord. We keep on teaching God's Word and pray for hearts to be changed. I've seen it happen. Oh, and while we are at it, it would be well to evaluate our own hearts.

SELFISHNESS

Nothing defines evangelism like the word *selflessness*. To win a soul to the Lord often means a person who has absolutely nothing to gain personally, is putting himself on the line for the sake of another. A selfish heart works for what it can get. A Christlike heart works for what it can give. You show me a successful soul-winner and I will show you an unselfish man or woman. Paul wrote to the Corinthians, "...For I am not seeking my own good, but the good of many, so that they may be saved" (I Corinthians 10:33).

I hope I am completely off base, but it seems to me that our culture is becoming more and more self-centered. Maybe that is happening in our churches. Have we given people the wrong message by becoming so inwardly focused? Could that be one of the chief reasons we are seeing less evangelism? Do we in the church need to be putting greater emphasis on reaching out to others and less on ministering to ourselves?

Many years ago, when I was leading a visitation program, my last statement to our visitation people each week before leaving with their assignments was almost always the same. The message was, "You are doing for the people you are about to visit the most important thing anyone has ever done for them." Maybe some of our churches need a heart transplant. A heart full of love would be good. It is love that produces the selflessness that will enable us to point some to Heaven.

FOR YOUR CONSIDERATION

1. Do you know anyone who obviously has the gift of evangelism?

2. What does the author mean when he states that evangelism is *a disciple thing*?

3. What is the significance of Luke 10:2 to evangelism?

4. When was the last time you asked someone, "Do you know Jesus as your personal savior?"

5. Is it possible for an extroverted person to be shy?

6. What are three things we can do to help us overcome the fear of doing evangelism?

7. What is courage? How does that relate to our practice of evangelism?

8. Is there really a difference between sloth and laziness?

9. What forms can sloth take as it relates to evangelism?

10. Are churches becoming more inwardly focused? Why do you say that?

CHAPTER 3

EVANGELISM AND CHURCH LEADERSHIP

There is an old story about a man who rode his Harley into a small town. He got off his motorcycle to walk over to where two men were sitting on a bench in front of a store. "Have you guys seen a group of riders wearing black helmets and leather jackets decorated with dragons pass through?" he asked.

"They came through about fifteen minutes ago. Hardly slowed down, at all," the man wearing the baseball cap declared. "You trying to catch them?" he asked.

"Yeah," the motorcycle jockey turned back to reply as he was already running toward his cycle, pulling his helmet onto his head, "I'm their leader."

"The other gentleman on the bench, who had remained silent up until now, looked at his partner with a puzzled expression, pushed his straw hat back on his head before saying, "Seems to me it would be hard to lead from fifteen minutes back."

QUALITIES NEEDED FOR EVANGELISTIC LEADERSHIP

Motivated leadership is crucial to accomplishing just about anything. Evangelism is no exception. When competent leaders are out front, leading the way, much will be accomplished. No committed leadership – little or no results. One longtime Bible college professor told me, "Our evangelism problem is a leadership problem." Could he be right? Is the work of evange-lism diminishing, to a large degree, because of the lack of people to lead that work? Let me suggest eight qualities needed by such leaders. Perhaps you can add to the list.

1. An evangelistic leader will have a passion for souls. He/she will genuinely care about people.
2. An evangelistic leader will be open to other disciples around him about his concern.
3. An evangelistic leader will involve himself in the work of pointing people to Christ. He will model evangelism that people can emulate.
4. An evangelistic leader will take every opportunity to get training for the task.
5. An evangelistic leader will have strong convictions about Heaven and Hell as described in the Bible.
6. An evangelistic leader will live a life that will back up his/her message. An effective witness requires more than let-ting our lights shine. I once heard someone say that no one's light is that bright. That is true, but what we say must be backed up by our lives.
7. An evangelistic leader is one who has the capacity for keeping on.
8. An evangelistic leader will love and respect the Word of God.

WHERE TO FIND LEADERS

Let's consider four places from which leadership must arise if evangelism is to be a successful endeavor for the church. *Obviously, leaders for evangelism must emerge from the pulpit.* I have never known of a successful evangelistic church that did not have a man in the pulpit who talked it up and lived it. The church that turns out a constant flow of soul-winners will almost always be led by a preacher who, himself, is an example of one who takes seriously the Lord's commission to evangelize lost sinners. He will be the chief motivator and will speak often from the pulpit of the task.

Does that even need to be stated? Everyone knows that pastors are the chief soul-winners in the church. That certainly should be the case, but is it? I have spent much of my adult life as a minister. I love and admire preachers. There is no group of people I respect more, but the fact is, one does not automatically become an evangelistic leader by virtue of being called to a pulpit. That kind of leadership must come out of the heart. Let me suggest some factors that can hamper the man in the pulpit from being the evangelistic leader he needs to be.

1. He may come to the position without adequate teaching and training on the subject. The preacher is usually a product of his formal and/or informal ministerial education. Perhaps his education for the ministry did not include practical lessons in this matter.

2. The preacher may be caught-up with other responsibilities. He will be assigned several tremendously important duties. Sermons must be prepared. Hospital visitation is not an option for most preachers. There is counseling and administration to be done and much more. One man of God that I respect highly gave me the rule I tried to live by in my years of pastoral ministry. He told me "There are some things for which we must find the time. At the top of that list is evangelism." Some things can be put off. Soul-winning is not one of those. The beautiful thing about it is that much evangelism can be accomplished as we go about those other tasks. I mentioned in an earlier chapter that Reggie Thomas was my instructor for personal evangelism in my freshman year of college. Mr. Thomas, at that time, was minister of the large East Point Christian Church. He

once told his class that when he was called to that church, he knew that such matters as administration, counseling, and hospital visitation would occupy much of his time. Before beginning that ministry, he said he committed to the Lord that he would hold at least one afternoon and one evening of every week for evangelistic visitation. The wisdom of that decision was seen week after week as people gave their lives to Jesus during his ministry with that church.

3. The preacher can become pre-occupied with lesser chores. If one is not careful, he can fall into the trap of spending the bulk of his time on that which interests him most or maybe the activities easiest for him. The preacher may be a gourmet cook, but he should not be tied down to preparing church dinners. Perhaps he is a master carpenter, but the building of walls around the church needs to be left to others. There is absolutely nothing wrong with investing time in such activities, if it doesn't take away from more important responsibilities such as evangelism. I often hear preachers complain about their lack of time due to all the hats they wear. Priorities need to be set with the Word of God in one hand. That list should be jealously honored.

4. It is possible that the man called to the pulpit simply does not have a heart for evangelism. It may be harsh, but I would go a step beyond most and say, he should not be leading a church if he is not strongly convinced of the necessity of such work. I might suggest there could be a place for him on a church staff if I did not take the hard-core position of insisting that every paid staff member of the church, in some way, be involved in the evangelistic effort of the church. I would not insist that the pastor have the gift of evangelism, most do not. But I would expect him to have a deep commitment to that work.

It is true that the evangelistic strategies of various men in the pulpit will differ depending upon their strengths, abilities, and opportunities. It isn't so much which methods are used, as it is that *some* method be incorporated. Paul exhorted the young preacher Timothy, ...do the work of an evangelist, discharge all the duties of your ministry" (2 Timothy 4:5).

In addition to the pulpit, leaders for evangelism should be found in the boardroom. The church that would be evangelistic needs to have people among their "lay leadership" who recognize the biblical place of evangelism in the work of the church. That is true regardless of the administrational intricacies the group embraces. The work will be stifled if there are no people to stand up for evangelism when decisions are made, and planning is done. That can be accomplished in two ways: either by adding people to the leadership team who meet that requirement, or by educating those who are already in place.

Sometimes, leadership for the churches evangelistic endeavors can come from the pew. There were times in my own ministry when the number one supporter for evangelism wasn't a staff member or even part of the church lay leadership team. I learned long ago that some of the most effective leaders in our churches do not necessarily hold an "official" leadership position. That may be truer regarding evangelism than with most other aspects of the church's work. I remember a preacher friend telling me about a gentleman coming into their church. That middle-aged man never filled any "official" leadership position. However, he had a heart for souls and the small church quadrupled its evangelistic results due to that man's leadership.

The fourth place I would suggest we look for evangelistic leadership is in the children and youth departments of our churches. The way to assure the future of the evangelistic church is to teach and train young people in our midst on the subject. Evangelistic leaders can be raised up. Don't underestimate this source. It's easier to mold the attitudes of young people than to change the mindset of adults.

I was a sophomore in high school when I accepted the Lord. My friend, Joe, a year older than me, had a great deal to do with my making that decision. We heard a lot about evangelism in our youth group, and I remember our preacher, Dave Carnine, once teaching our high school group how to lead one to Jesus. By the time I left that group, I had some strong convictions about soul-winning and a little bit of know-how. I am sure my youth group experience has a lot to do with why evangelism has been an important concern for me throughout my adult life.

THE LEADERSHIP OF A STRONG NATIONAL VOICE

There were many people in the little church where I attended as a high school student who blessed my life—eqspecially the men of the congregation. I was looking for a father figure and I found more than one. Several of those men were heroes to me. I loved them with all my heart. The names of several of them appear on my ordination certificate, and I take great pride in that. All of those who signed that certificate have gone to be with the Lord. That is why I can write this section. If I had written it while they were still with us, they probably would have lifted the document that certifies me as a preacher of the gospel. You see, they did not think highly of evangelist Billy Graham. Much of the world revered him, but not these good men. Why? I think mostly for two reasons. First, they had some doctrinal differences with him. One difference had to do with salvation, and they could not abide that. The other reason is that they objected to some of his methods. I don't think that would have been a big problem if they had been correctly informed rather than listening to hearsay.

There is absolutely no doubt in my mind that I would have been in deep trouble with those great men of God, had they heard me say, "We desperately need another national evangelistic leader like Billy Graham." Billy Graham was the man who kept reminding us that evangelism is a priority for the Christian. He successfully carried the banner of evangelism across denominational barriers for almost half a century. I wonder, is the work of evangelism gradually eroding, at least in part, because there is no strong national voice calling us to that work? I know he did not do it alone. Other evangelists and strong evangelistic preachers stood firm and worked long and hard, but the call of that national voice that people respected made a huge difference. Could we join in praying that God would raise up another servant who could nurture our awareness for evangelism? Is there someone out there that God could use even as he used Graham for all those years?

FOR YOUR CONSIDERATION

1. What do you feel are the three most important qualities for an evangelistic leader?

2. Where are some of the places from which evangelistic leaders can be pulled?

3. Can you site three factors that might cause the man in the pulpit to be ill-equipped to lead the church's evangelism program?

4. Why does an evangelistic leader need to have the capacity for keeping on?

5. Is it true that a preacher might sometimes have to decide between doing a good or a necessary chore?

6. How do you feel about a man with no heart for evangelism occupying the pulpit?

7. Is it possible for a "lay person" to give leadership to the church's evangelistic efforts?

8. Is it appropriate to train church youth for leadership in evangelism?

9. Who is a person you know that you feel has the potential to be a leader in the work of evangelism?

10. How can a strong national voice aid the work of evangelism? Do you see such a voice on the horizon?

CHAPTER 4

EVANGELISM AND BASIC THEOLOGY

The word *theology*, unfortunately, is not a word that will cause most Christians to jump with excitement. I am told that polls show what I have observed. There is a diminishing awareness and interest in theology among evangelicals. The word *theology* actually comes from two Greek words that, combined, mean "the study of God." So Christian theology is simply an attempt to understand God as He is revealed in the Bible. Our theology – how we understand God and his teaching, will drastically affect how we live and act. One's theology will dictate how he responds to our Lord's commission. The place of evangelism in the church, and among Christians in general, can be greatly enhanced or hampered by shifting theological thought. Numerous points of theology could be discussed here, but we will hold it to three that are probably most affecting the church's ability to carry out its God-given purpose of evangelizing the world.

THE BIBLE AS THE INFALLIBLE, INERRANT WORD OF GOD

Is the Bible a true and accurate revelation of the will of God as it claims? Paul wrote to the young preacher Timothy, "All Scripture is God-breathed and useful for teaching, rebuking, correction, and training in righteousness, so that the servant of God may be thoroughly equipped for every good work" (2 Timothy

3:16-17). That settles it for many of us. Scripture comes from the very mouth of God. It is the infallible, inerrant Word of God. Most of the brethren with whom I worship and fellowship tell me they believe that. But I am finding more and more that they don't understand it quite the same way I do. There was a time when if we said we believed the Bible is inspired of God, there was little doubt we meant all the Bible was God's infallible message by which He intended us to live. It doesn't always mean that today. We talk about matters such as the nature and extent of Bible inspiration.

Ironically, that person who claims to believe the Bible is God-inspired may also believe it's not quite up to snuff when it comes to history, science, or even doctrine. If we questioned them, they might remind us the Bible was written in a different time and a different culture. They perhaps would talk of standards that have changed. They might tell us that God led the writers to include some of his ideas, but those scribes also included their own thoughts. The bottom line is that when we start picking apart God's Word, we are likely to eliminate those sections we don't much like. If obedience to a portion of the Bible is difficult for us, we can find a way to rationalize it. In my mind, if one takes away the inspiration of the Bible, he is, for all practical purposes, taking away the motivation for evangelism.

What motivates one to participate in evangelism? It is part of the Lord's plan. It is a positive response to the Lord's instructions. Where do we find those instructions, and why should they be taken seriously? Why, the commission is right there in the Bible. What does that matter if the Bible or that part of the Bible is not from God?

We can be motivated to evangelize by our genuine concern for the souls of people. Where does the idea of salvation through Jesus come from anyway? It's there, in the Bible. But what if the Bible is less than the inspired Word of God? Are you beginning to see why I am suggesting that the weakening of the doctrine of

Bible inspiration can negatively affect our desire to carry out the Lord's commission?

Have you ever known anyone to suggest, "Want to have some real fun tonight? Let's go soul-winning! Nothing beats that for a good time." Not a statement you are likely to hear. People attempt to win souls because they have been convicted by God's Word to do so. The word of God speaks to them about his will and the souls of the lost. You take away the authority of the Word and you take away most of the motivation for evangelism.

PLURALISM

Perhaps it has risen out of our desire to be politically correct. Maybe we just like leaving the impression on our fellow man that we are tolerant. I don't know the reasons, but I am alarmed by the unbiblical and dangerous doctrine of pluralism that is rapidly raising its head in Christian circles. Pluralism is the belief that there are multiple paths to God. It encourages the idea that there are many sources one might tap to find salvation. It carries the idea that the many gods are really one. The pluralist would argue that one way is best for some people while another might be best for others. It is a doctrine that at best limits the work of Jesus as Savior.

What does the Bible say about this matter? The writer of Hebrews says of Jesus, "Although he was a son, he learned obedience from what he suffered and, once made perfect, he became the source of eternal salvation for all who obey him" (Hebrews 5:8-9). Notice that the writer did not say Jesus became *a* source of eternal salvation. He became *the* source of eternal salvation.

Jesus made the same statement to his disciples about Himself. "Jesus answered, 'I am the way and the truth and the life. No one comes to the Father except through me,'" (John 14:6) Jesus did not say, "I am *a* way" or "*one of the ways.* He said, *I am the way.* Jesus clearly states He is the only way to God, the Father. That is the only position that one can take when he accepts the Bible as the inspired Word of God. Paul assures us in 1 Timothy 2:5, "For there is one God and one mediator between God and mankind, the man Christ Jesus, who gave himself as a ransom for all men..." The way to Heaven is through Jesus alone.

If there are many gods or many ways of getting to God, why should we bother to attempt to lead anyone to Jesus. If there are many ways to get there, we can let our friend find his own way in his own time. It is not really important that he know about Jesus. There is no reason or urgency for us to sacrifice our time and effort to tell anyone about Jesus if there is nothing special about Him. But, of course, Jesus is special. He is the way to God. We must tell as many people as possible of him and his love.

It is recorded in Acts 4:1-12. It happened in Jerusalem. Peter and John were brought before the high priest and other important officials. Their crime? They healed a cripple and dared to teach the people and "proclaim in Jesus the resurrection of the dead." They were asked by those officials, "By what power did you do this?" Peter told them, "It is by the name of Jesus Christ of Nazareth, whom you crucified but whom God raised from the dead, that this man stands before you healed." Peter went on to say, "He is the stone you builders rejected, which has become the capstone. Salvation is found in no one else, for there is no other name under heaven given to men by which we must be saved" (Acts 4:11-12).

Did you catch that? "Salvation is found in no one else." Why is salvation found in only Jesus? He is the only one who could offer a perfect sacrifice for our sins. Anyone else would have to die for his own sins, but Jesus had no sin. He was divine, but he lived on earth as man. He rose on the third day after his death. He is the only person ever to die and come back on his own to ascend into heaven. All other religious leaders and important non-religious figures who have lived and died through the years are still in their graves. Jesus, the one in whom salvation is found is still alive. It's an honor to have the opportunity to point others to Him.

THE REALITY OF HELL

I haven't heard many of my Christian friends deny that Hell exists. Though I do occasionally hear one of them suggest that a loving God would not send anyone to a horrible place of eternal torment. However, the problem is, I seldom hear Hell spoken of at all. Preachers don't preach about it much anymore, and teachers find ways to exclude it from their lessons. I think we just ignore it and pretend it's not in the Bible. But it is in the Bible. Let me say upfront that no one goes to Hell because God wants him to be there. 2 Peter 3:9 should settle that. "The Lord is not slow in keeping his promise, as some understand slowness. He is patient with you, not wanting anyone to perish, but everyone to come to repentance."

Many people tell us they believe in Heaven, but not Hell. The reality is that the Bible speaks a great deal more about Hell than Heaven. A study of the Gospels will reveal Jesus speaking much of the nature of Hell. In Mark 9:43, He speaks of it as a place "where the fire never goes out." The Lord describes it in Matthew 25:46 as a place of eternal punishment. In Mark 9:48, according to Jesus it is "where the worm does not die, and the fire is not quenched." In Matthew 8:12, it is said by the Lord to be a place of weeping and gnashing of teeth. And in Matthew 25:30, Jesus points out it is a place of darkness.

Much more concerning, the nature of Hell can be found in Scripture. Perhaps you'll want to get your concordance off the shelf and take a look. R.G. Lee, a mighty pulpiteer and a great evangelist from days gone by wrote a poem entitled "Hell, the Prisonhouse of Despair:"

Hell the prisonhouse of despair
Here are some things that will be there.
Fire and brimstone are there we know
For God in His word hath told us so.
Memory, remorse, suffering and pain
Weeping and wailing, but all in vain.
Blasphemers, swearers, haters of God
Christ rejectors, while here they trod.
Murders, gamblers, drunkards and liars-
Will have their part in the Lake of Fire.
The filthy, the vile, the cruel, and the mean
What a horrible mob in hell will be seen!

The worse part of Hell is that those who are there will be separated from Christ. Paul revealed in 2 Thessalonians 1:8-9, "He will punish those who do not know God and do not obey the gospel of our Lord Jesus. They will be punished with everlasting destruction and shut out from the presence of the Lord and from the glory of his might." Revelation 20:14-15 relates John's vision of that coming day, "Then death and Hades were thrown into the Lake of Fire. The Lake of Fire is the second death. Anyone whose name was not found written in the book of life was thrown into the lake of fire."

How can we not have a strong commitment to reaching out to our family and friends with the Gospel when we are convicted that Hell is real? How can we rest knowing that it will be the final eternal destination of those who do not know Jesus? Can we turn our backs on those whose names are not written in the book of life? It's an old idea, but perhaps if we would spend a little time studying the biblical subject of Hell, we would find ourselves more persuaded of the need for evangelism. Maybe a little more attention to the reality of Hell will enhance our evangelistic efforts. I read that someone admitted, "Yes evangelism is hard, but it's harder to know our friends and family are burning in Hell."

FOR YOUR CONSIDERATION

1. How do you understand the word *theology?*

2. How is it possible for our theology to affect how we live and act?

3. What does the term *inerrancy* mean to you?

4. To what extent do you accept the inspiration of the Bible?

5. How can belief about the inspiration of the Bible affect one's evangelistic effort?

6. What is theological pluralism? How prevalent is it in Christian circles?

7. How does theological pluralism affect the work of evangelism?

8. Is Hell a real place? How does the Bible portray it?

9. How can our acceptance and concept of Hell affect our evangelistic efforts?

10. How do some other basic Bible doctrines relate to the work of evangelism?

CHAPTER 5

SOME MISCONCEPTIONS ABOUT EVANGELISM

The practice of evangelism, as we have already determined, can mean stepping outside one's comfort zone. It can be excruciatingly hard and time consuming for some. It likely will require a real commitment. Perhaps for that reason, we may look for ways to excuse our lack of involvement. The search for such justification can lead to acceptance of certain assumptions that are no more than half truths at best. Let's consider four misconceptions that may sound good and perhaps contain measures of truth but in fact, if accepted as unqualified fact, can cripple the important work to which the Lord called us.

MISCONCEPTION #1 – GROWING ATTENDANCE CONSTITUTES EVANGELISM

As a young man breaking into the ministry, I became acquainted with Elmer Towns' little book, *The Ten Largest Sunday Schools in America*. Other books like *The Ten Fastest Growing Sunday Schools in America* followed. The Church Growth Movement was underway, and I, like many churchmen in America, was hooked. We were obsessed — attendance growth at any cost! We bought old school buses to transport children to our Sunday schools. We planned big days in which we doubled and tripled our attendance for the day. We dreamed of someday breaking into that top ten.

We called it evangelism. "Lay leaders" read those books too, and it became a rather precarious time for preachers. Leaders, not seeing their churches attain the kind of growth they were reading about, were sometimes quick to pull the plug on their preachers to look for someone who could get the job done. For many, booming church attendance had become the bottom line. Church attendance rapidly became an end in itself. Since that time the church growth emphasis has taken several different turns, but the concept that larger numbers in the pews constitutes getting the job done has persisted. Getting people to church isn't easy, but it's less complicated and stressful than leading them to the Lord.

Don't misunderstand me. Rising church attendance is a good thing. For all the years I was a preacher, I diligently labored for good attendance. I was encouraged by growing numbers and discouraged when they were down. Attendance brings people into worship. People are exposed to God's word. It can aid evangelism by providing prospects. I don't think it is true now, but for years I felt that if I could get someone to attend church for three or four consecutive Lord's days, I could win them to the Lord. The point here is that while church attendance might be growing, we still haven't necessarily evangelized those who are attending. The job is not finished. We have not evangelized them until they have come to know Jesus as Lord and Savior. There is a saying that has bounced around for years that says, "the main thing is to keep the main thing the main thing." When we focus on evangelism as our ultimate goal, and church attendance as part of the process, we are keeping the main thing the main thing. To consider the task complete when we draw big numbers to our services means we have forgotten the main thing. Getting people in church is a step in the right direction, but it is short of evangelizing those people.

MISCONCEPTION #2 — ALL CHURCH WORK IS ACTUALLY EVANGELISM

One might tell us, "I am doing my evangelism by cooking the Wednesday night meal or by doing the repair work on the church plumbing. As a preacher who struggled to keep cooks in the kitchen on Wednesday nights and often had to deal with defective plumbing in the church facilities, I greatly appreciate such people. They are doing important jobs that certainly aid the Lord's work. I do not take lightly their contributions, but they are not doing evangelism. Oh, you might argue, there is a sense in which they are making an evangelistic contribution. There might be a grain of validity to your statement. If the church has confined itself to evaluating all its programs by their effectiveness in accomplishing the Lord's commission, then strictly speaking, any job in the church would be a contribution to disciple-making. Though it carries an element of truth, that is stretching the point pretty far. All too often we may excuse ourselves from the Lord's call to seek the lost by claiming we are doing our part by driving the church van for youth trips to the bowling alley.

For the last three or four years I have written inspirational mystery novels. These stories are filled with godly truths and biblical principles to live by. I might tell you that has been my contribution to evangelism during those years. To be honest, I don't know of one person who has come to know the Lord by reading the Davis Morgan Mysteries. Some have learned certain truths that they needed to learn. Some of the readers have a better understanding of particular Christian principles and, according to the reports I have received, a good number have been entertained with clean, wholesome, and sometimes exciting stories. But I don't know of one person who has come to know the Lord by reading one of those books. Does that mean it has been a useless effort and I should stop writing those stories? No, not necessarily. However, it does mean that I cannot call my writing evangelism. I cannot conscientiously claim that any evangelistic responsibilities I have are being fulfilled by my writing ministry. My writing is one thing and my evangelistic work is another.

How many people are justifying their lack of involvement in the Lord's call to evangelize with a declaration that their commitment to that work is being satisfied by some job they are doing that is commendable, but has little or nothing to do with evangelism? Why should they get involved in evangelism when in their minds, they are already evangelizing? It's called rationalization.

MISCONCEPTION #3 – WE CAN DO OUR EVANGELISM BY DEMONSTRAITING A GODLY LIFE

"My contribution to doing evangelism is that I live a godly life," a friend recent declared in my presence. I commend my friend and the many others who I have heard make similar statements through the years. Their propensity for living a life in conformity with God's will is wonderful. Every Christian should do likewise. But, while faithful living enhances one's ability to evangelize, it is not equivalent to evangelism. How we live is a foundation for evangelism, but not a substitute for it.

We often use the word *witness* when speaking of sharing Jesus. When one is put on a witness stand, he is required to speak. When he is asked a question, he is not allowed to remain silent and simply point to his good life. An exemplary life will surely back up his witness, making it more believable, but he has not testified until he opens his mouth and says something. One may back up his Christian witness with a quality life, but until he speaks of Jesus, he has not given testimony.

I have heard several speakers on various occasions make statements from the pulpit about the superiority of Christian living over spoken words as related to evangelism. In each case, I appreciated what the preachers had to say. They were simply attempting to emphasize how important the right kind of life is to winning people to the Lord. However, I wondered about the chorus of *amens* that seemingly always follow. Were the *amens* a response to the intended message, or were they the joyful reactions of a people who felt they had been let off the hook? Did they believe the preacher was telling them they were not expected to speak out for Jesus? Did they think the preacher was saying they only had to live the life Jesus expected of them?

I'm all about living a life that will give credibility to our words, but such a life does not eliminate our responsibility to tell the good news of Jesus and his love everywhere we have opportunity. A godly life is a good starting place, but from there, we go on to equip ourselves to speak the gospel message.

MISCONCEPTION #4 – REORGANIZING THE KINGDOM IS EVANGELISM

The churches with which I am affiliated are extremely strong in Indianapolis. In fact, there are more in this city than in any other area in the country. When I ministered in the suburbs, it wasn't unusual for me to receive a Monday morning phone call from Don Sharpe or one of my other preacher friends in the area telling me that a person or family from my congregation had placed membership with his church. And it wasn't unusual for me to make such a Monday morning call. You see, some of our members seemed always to find a reason for moving on after a year or two within a particular church. Some of them tried and found lacking six or eight of our brotherhood churches as time passed. Some eventually went on to other kinds of churches. That is probably not a good practice, but it is the prerogative of one if he so chooses.

I would suggest it is a mistake to call such additions to the church evangelism. Evangelism is reaching the unchurched, not the dissatisfied churched. It is reaching the lost, not latching on to those looking for better children's programing. Evangelism is not the work of rearranging the kingdom. It is the work of enlarging the Lord's kingdom.

We can, no doubt, make a valid argument for aggressively reaching out to the one who was once churched, but is now drifting with no spiritual ties or direction. Those people need to be reached and brought back into a fellowship where they can receive spiritual encouragement and guidance. I have often found that such people, despite their past affiliation, are actually in need of conversion. We dare not turn away anyone seeking refuge in our spiritual family. We are compelled to minister to all who allow us to do so. Making disciples of the spiritual drifters may be an untidy way of doing it, but it is all part of the Lord's work. It is, however, evangelism — reaching the lost on which we would do well to focus.

SO, WHAT SPECIFICLY IS EVANGELISM?

We have said evangelism is not building church attendance. It is not any church work we happen to be doing, nor is it simply living a Godly life. It is not rearranging the kingdom by moving Christians from church to church. Then what is evangelism? How should it be understood? One dictionary definition I came across is that "evangelism is the spreading of the Christian gospel by public preaching or personal witness." That says it pretty well.

I adore two descriptions of evangelism I have read. Leith Anderson wrote, "The simple definition of evangelism; Those who know, telling those who don't." How is that for keeping it simple, but still all inclusive?

For many years I have seen D.T. Niles's words on plaques and other places. Those striking words are, "Evangelism is just one beggar telling another beggar where to find bread." It's hard to say it better than that.

I have always thought of evangelism as first sharing why one needs Jesus, secondly, sharing how one comes to know Jesus, and thirdly, asking that one to receive Jesus. A critical mistake is to take the first two steps without including the third.

FOR YOUR CONSIDERATION

1. How can interpreting the building of church attendance as evangelism cripple the work of evangelism?

2. Is pushing church attendance a good thing or bad? Why?

3. What popular Christian books are most affecting the work of the church today? For good or for bad?

4. What is the logic behind the position that all church work is evangelism? Do you agree or disagree?

5. How are living a godly life and evangelism connected?

6. Does the fact they are connected mean that by living the life, one has done evangelism?

7. What do we mean by *reorganizing the kingdom?*

8. Would you consider reorganizing the kingdom to be evangelism? Why or why not?

9. How would you define or describe evangelism?

10. What elements do you understand to be involved in evangelism?

CHAPTER 6

SEVEN SIGNIFICANT THOUGHTS FOR EFFECTIVE EVANGELISM

In order to include everything, I would like to say, I probably would need to do around thirty chapters. A book of that magnitude, however, probably would not be used the way I want this book to be used. The alternative is to include a couple of chapters in which I share some *bullet* thoughts that otherwise would have been chapters. Here are seven of those thoughts.

LEARN TO LOVE PEOPLE AND HATE SIN

Jesus knew the cross was near. Moments earlier He washed the feet of his disciples and predicted his betrayal. He said to his anxious followers, "My children, I will be with you only a little longer. You will look for me, and just as I told the Jews, so I tell you now: Where I am going you cannot come. A new command I give you: Love one another. As I have loved you, so you must love one another. By this everyone will know that you are my disciples, if you love one another" (John 13:33-35).

People will be drawn to a Savior who has such an effect on his people. They will want what they see in those who have been touched by him. That love will not be confined to the circle of the redeemed. It will stretch out to all mankind. That is the way of Christ's love when it reaches maturity. It is that love that will be the heart and soul of evangelism. Effective evangelism does not result from a burning desire to build a large church. It does not spring out of someone's salesmanship ability. I have never seen a successful evangelistic effort succeed because someone beat a group of people into involvement. Effective evangelism is rooted in love for Christ, love for people, and a hatred of sin that put Jesus on the cross and destroys the very people we love.

What is the very first step to successful evangelism? It is the presence of love. When people love with the love of God, we will have no problem getting them to share the gospel message. And when the lost come face to face with that love which compels us, many of them will want to experience such love for themselves. I have often said, "get the love right and most everything else seems to fall into place."

PARTNER WITH THE HOLY SPIRIT

"I can't do that!" I couldn't tell you how many times I have heard people make that statement concerning evangelism.

I always want to respond, and sometimes do with, "I know you can't, and neither can I. We have a sufficient power beyond ourselves upon which we can depend to work through us." Jesus told his disciples, "When you are brought before synagogues, rulers, and authorities, do not worry about how you will defend yourselves or what you will say, for the Holy Spirit will teach you at that time what you should say" (Luke 12:11-12).

Isn't it encouraging to know that One lives within us who has the power to put the right words into our mouths? You may correctly respond, "He's not talking about evangelism here. He's speaking of their defense." Let's look at Acts 1:8, "But you will receive power when the Holy Spirit comes on you, and you will be my witnesses in Jerusalem, and in all Judea and Samaria, and to the ends of the earth."

We are equipped for evangelism by virtue of receiving the indwelling of God's Holy Spirit at the time of our conversion (Acts 2:38). We simply need to open ourselves up to Him and allow

Him to work in our lives. Much of the evangelism in which I have participated through the years has been a two by two approach, but there has been a third party involved Who has not been seen. He has been the most important person on the team. He's there to pick up the slack when we are struggling. I have experienced that numerous times through the years.

DEVELOP A "GO" MENTALITY

I realize that to develop a "go" mentality is the opposite of what we are often hearing today. We sometimes hear pastors of churches, especially large, popular churches, explain, "Our approach to evangelism is not to go out into the highways and byways, but rather to offer the best we can offer, and compel the people to come. No doubt, if approached correctly, it can work for the church that has the resources and reputation to make it work. While the mega church can embrace that philosophy and probably pull it off, most country, small town, and struggling churches cannot make it work very well. If they are to reach people, they will need to go get them.

One of the problems arising from this is when the young preacher, just starting his ministry, who is petrified at the idea of knocking on doors, hears it and is ecstatic. *You mean I don't have to do visitation in order to reach people? I can simply open the doors and say "come."* Do you think he is going out to knock on doors? Do you think he will organize any kind of evangelistic outreach program? No, he will open the doors and say "come," and he will feel justified in doing so because of what he heard from a well-regarded church builder. In most of those cases, few if any will be reached. I wish well-intentioned pastors and seminar leaders could understand the damage they are doing to those ministries with such statements.

For many years, I have heard it said by some "scholars" that when Jesus gave the Great Commission, instructing his disciples to "go and make disciples," the original text can also mean "as you go." Those scholars would imply the text offers no specific instructions to make a special effort to *go* for the express purpose of making disciples. The commission, they would tell us, is to make disciples as you go. I suppose it is true that it can be interpreted either way or perhaps both ways, but I choose to read it as Bible translators have chosen to translate it all through the years — "Go." I believe, in most cases we will be most successful with our evangelistic efforts when we develop a *go* mentality.

LEARN TO WORK WITH A POLITE PERSISTENCE

I have seen in my lifetime a gradual hardening of the heart toward the gospel. I don't know if it was easier to win people to the Lord in the early stages of my evangelistic involvement, but I believe most people were more ready to hear what we had to say in those days. Perhaps, had it not been for my own clumsiness and dependence on self, I would have seen better results. It is the influence of the world in which we now live that leads to the hardening of many a heart against the gospel. The world is busy constructing walls that make our work more difficult. For that reason, success requires we be prepared to persist in our effort to reach the lost individual.

It often takes many contacts to break through that heart of cement to reach one for Jesus. I don't mean we should obnoxiously keep forcing ourselves on anyone. However, we must work to keep the door open and the talks alive. We would do well to remember it is the eternal soul of the person for which we are competing. And it is a competition; because, Satan is doing everything he can to keep the prospect under his influence.

This evangelistic persistence of ours must be polite in nature. The Christian must be a lady or gentleman in every respect. People should be glad when we show up. Hopefully, they think enough of us to open the door and not sic the dog on us when they see us coming. The successful soul-winner will earn the right to witness to his friend by his/her gentle concern. One who understands we care, can probably be won. It has often been said that people don't care about what we have to say until they know we care. May we successfully allow our persistence in the life of a lost sinner to be a sign to him that we really do care.

GET TRAINING

We briefly spoke of this in an earlier chapter, but I need to add a few remarks about evangelistic training. When I conducted visitation programs, I started by recruiting and bringing people into a classroom setting to learn how to do what I was asking them to do. With each phase, I recruited a few who would not only learn in the classroom, but also by live participation with those already taught. They would be sent out as *silent partners* to see demonstrated what they were learning. I did not ask for volunteers. I recruited the best people available. It has long been my belief that people are likely to perform in the same way they are recruited. If their services are secured in a three-minute haphazard effort between Sunday School and worship, they probably will not take the job seriously. If one comes to their home with a well-prepared presentation in which they are assured they are needed, they are more likely to give their best effort to that job.

In the classes, the recruits were required to learn the material and were tested each step of the way. As the leader, I would demonstrate, for the class members, the use of the material as it was taught. Finally, each person would, themselves, do the soul-winning presentation in the presence of their classmates. It was always a big day when the students got that behind them. Usually, they not only were ready to put it to use but were chomping at the bit to do so. I am sure there are other ways of doing the training, but this is what we did. And it worked for us.

Regardless of how we go about it, the training is necessary. To send one out for such work without preparation is to doom him or her to failure. Would we put someone in an elementary school classroom without any teacher education? To do so would be a disaster for both the teacher and the students. No less is true of the personal evangelist. I remind you again that we are talking about people's eternal souls. How can we not do our best to prepare people to get the job done?

So, what if you want to do the work of evangelism, but your church has no evangelistic program or training. What can you do? Don't let that discourage you. Find someone of like mind and team up with him/her. Locate some material that would help you prepare for the task and thoroughly study it until you have learned it. The last few chapters of this little book will be practical in nature. It might give you what you need to get started. Spend some time praying with your partner and pick out a couple of people for whom you are concerned. Then get started.

HANG WITH THE UNCHURCHED

How will we encourage the lost to become Christians if we aren't acquainted with any people outside the Lord? Jesus was constantly criticized by the religious leaders of his day for his association with tax collectors and sinners. Jesus responded to them when they condemned Him for being with Matthew, a tax collector, and his friends, "It is not the healthy who need a doctor, but the sick" (Matthew 9:12).

I love the Lord's words in Matthew 18:12-14, "What do you think? If a man owns a hundred sheep, and one of them wanders away, will he not leave the ninety-nine on the hills and go to look for the one that wandered off? And if he finds it, truly I tell you, he is happier about that one sheep than about the ninety-nine that did not wander off. In the same way, your Father in heaven is not willing that any of these little ones should perish." Evangelism is an attempt to bring back the lost sheep.

It is true we are warned by scripture to be careful about involvement in the world. We can put ourselves in great spiritual peril by friendship with the world system that opposes the Lord. We need fellowship with those who would aid our spiritual growth. It becomes unmistakably clear that there is a balance to be found here. We need Christian friends, but if we would lead people to the Lord, we must locate and know them. Here is the guideline I have always tried to follow for myself. I constantly evaluate my friendships and my relationships with those with whom I tend to spend my time. If my evaluation reveals I am influencing the sinner more than he is affecting me, then I am relatively safe. I will continue to cultivate that friendship. If he is influencing me more than I him, then I will adjust or politely back off.

One of the reasons new Christians are such great sources for finding those in need of salvation is that they usually are fresh from an environment where most of their friends and associates were non-Christian. After we have been in the Lord for a time, we tend to draw our closest friends from within a pool of Christians. In one sense that is a good thing. We need such friendships.

It pays to search for sinners in need of salvation, but it's not wise to go to many of the places they go and do some of the things they do. It would be good to be a friend to Christians and sinners alike, but the wise man will keep a close eye on himself as well. We would do well to embrace the attitude of Paul who earlier in I Corinthians nine had spoken of becoming all things to all people, but then stated this caution in verse twenty-seven, "No, I beat my body and make it my slave so that after I have preached to others, I myself will not be disqualified for the prize."

STRIVE TO BE KNOWN FOR WHAT YOU SUPPORT

I understand that being for certain actions means automatically being against others. We must stand against what God is against. It is wrong to accept all things in the name of love. As Christians, there is no other choice but to stand for what God is for and against what God is against. But up for discussion here is the way in which that is approached.

It is my opinion that people are more likely to respond well to a person, church, or Savior they understand to be a positive influence in the world. They will listen when they conclude we have something to offer. We don't go out into the world to strike down all sin. That's the Lord's job. We go out to win people to Him. Hopefully, that will bring about the needed changes. It is not our focus to change all the evil practices in our culture. As much as we want it to change, we are not going to get very far if that is our goal. But as people come to know Jesus, society starts to change. It is our job to point people to the Lord. Our hope is they will be changed, thus changing the world of which they are part.

There are many practices that are prevalent and legal in our culture that I am strongly against. I do not back down from the biblical position, and I will do what I can to aid in changing the deficiencies I see. But I don't want to be known as an anti-anything. I want to be known for my pro-Christ position.

A while back when I was still an active pastor, I visited in a home where I introduced myself to the man of the house as the minister of the church I was serving at the time. His response to meeting me was, "Well, what are you against?'

I smiled at him and told him, "I'm not here to talk about what I am against, I'm here to tell you about Who I'm for." He seemed to like that, and we had a civilized discussion about things spiritual.

FOR YOUR CONSIDERATION

1. How does love aid evangelism?

2. What will the Holy Spirit do for us in the soul-winning process?

3. What does the author mean by *a "go" mentality*?

4. How do you interpret Jesus's statement in Matthew 28:19?

5. Why is persistence important in the work of evangelism?

6. What does a personal evangelist need to know to be successful?

7. What is likely to happen if one attempts to do the work of evangelism without training?

8. Why is it necessary that Christians spend time with non-Christians?

9. What kind of balance should a Christian strive for regarding his/her Christian and non-Christian friends?

10. Relating to evangelism, why is it profitable for one to be known for what he/she supports rather than what he/she is against?

SEVEN MORE SIGNIFICANT THOUGHTS FOR EFFECTIVE EVANGELISM

T o keep from leaving out anything important, here are seven more sharp points. The fact we are allotting little space to these subjects does not mean they are not important to doing our best work as the Lord's servants.

START WITH THE FAMILY

On occasion, I have heard people say, "I can talk with people I don't know well about Jesus, but I am not able to speak to family members about Him." I have wondered why that is the case. Shouldn't we be able to witness most effectively to those we know and love? Maybe it's because we are aware that they know the real us. Perhaps we are not confident that after what family members have seen up close in our lives, they will take us seriously. Regardless of the reason for such reluctance, we need to get over it. The natural place for us to begin our evangelistic effort is with family members who don't know the Lord. I believe family is best won through a low-key approach, supported by a godly life. In 1 Peter 3:1, 2, we find these words, "Wives, in the same way submit yourselves to your own husbands so that, if any of them do not believe the word, they may be won over without words by the behavior of their wives, when they see the purity and reverence of your lives."

The Apostle Paul speaks to dads, "Fathers, do not exasperate your children; instead, bring them up in the training and instruction of the Lord" (Ephesians 6:4). The instructions I find in scripture tell me that pointing immediate family members to the Lord starts by dedicating ourselves to our biblical role as a family member. Gentle instruction backed up by the proper life seems to be the way to go.

The fact is, our attempts to bring people other than family to the Lord will sometimes be affected by the spiritual status of our own family. I was once told by a gentleman, "One of your church members came by my home to talk with me about being a Christian. I told him he needed to get his own house in order before he tries to straighten out mine." There are times when such an evaluation of one's fitness for the job is totally inappropriate. For example, we may be doing everything we know to do, without success, to bring an adult son or daughter to faithfulness. When all is said and done, each adult is responsible for his/her own life. Sometimes, there may be past mistakes of which we have repented. We can change our ways, but we can't erase those earlier errors. The past should not keep us from doing today, what we can, to help people know the Lord.

PRAY EVANGELISTICLY

It was suggested to me that the typical prayer session at church sounds like the roll call at the local hospital. It is good to pray for those who are ill. We are exhorted in the Bible to do so. There are many situations that demand prayer support. Not long ago, a child asked me to pray for her missing dog. I prayed for her missing dog and was glad when it was found and brought home. There are many reasons to pray. Perhaps one area in which we need to strengthen our prayer efforts is concerning the lost. There is nothing people need more than to know Jesus as Lord and Savior. Why shouldn't we be praying for that to happen? Here are seven guidelines to making our prayers more evangelistic.

1. *Pray for, by name, those that are lost.* I remember well the preparation for the first evangelistic meeting in the little church I served right out of college. Two weeks before the series of meetings, we had five nights of prayer meetings in various homes. I took a list of fifteen people who needed to make decisions for the Lord to each of those meetings. Each night we prayed for those people by name. The week before the meeting started, we had five nights of visitation in which we visited with those fifteen people, encouraging them to make their decisions for Jesus. During the five nights of the meeting, thirteen of the fifteen responded at decision time to make decisions. It was no coincidence! Prayer followed by evangelism equals life and eternity changes.

2. *Pray for the workman.* The voice supported by prayer will likely see the most results. I sometimes recruited people to support specific people in our evangelism program with prayer.

3. *Undergird each individual effort with prayer.* It is good for evangelistic workers to go in pairs for several reasons. One of those reasons is that while the leader is speaking, the "silent partner" can be praying. I sometimes recruited several people, at another location, to be praying for a worker and prospect during the time the interview was taking place.

4. *Pray for the Lord to give us clear opportunities to speak about Him.* I think there were times in the early stages of my Christian life when I might have prayed the Lord would not put me in a position where I would have to do that.

That changed as time went on and I spiritually "manned-up" a bit.

5. *Pray for recognition of those opportunities when they come.* As I look back on my life, I see so many openings that came my way without my taking advantage of them. I regret that and often wonder how many people have gone into eternity without the Lord because I was blinded to the chances I was given.

6. *Pray that the Lord will help us to be at our best as his messengers.* We must not come to a place of self-reliance. We can only do our best when we realize that without the Lord's participation, we will never amount to very much in this work. It is a work that demands our best.

7. *Pray the Lord will raise up workers.* Will there ever be enough workers to cover the fields? I don't think so. Earlier we saw the words of Jesus in this matter, "He told them, 'The harvest is plentiful, but the workers are few. Ask the Lord of the harvest, therefore, to send out workers into his harvest field'" (Luke 10:2).

DON'T NEGLECT THE IMPORTANT

I, long ago, learned the trick for avoiding that which I do not want to do. It works like this: get busy with something more appealing. No one can criticize us for not doing their thing if we are obviously busy with something that is important to us. I trust committed Christians would not play that game with the important work to which the Lord has called us. However, when I have tried to recruit people to do evangelistic work, numerous people have responded to me with that familiar comeback, "I would like to do that, but I just don't have the time. I can't make the commitment you want me to make."

It may be true that we live in a world that offers far too many options. One of the extremely important skills for us to work on is correctly setting priorities. I once preached a sermon in which I made the statement, "Most of us find a way to do the things we really want to do." Boy, did I get in big trouble. It was probably one of the most unpopular sermons I ever presented. For a time, I was not looked on with great favor in those parts. I think we sometimes feel we are forced into certain activities when in reality, we have made the wrong decisions. Maybe we selected the less important pursuit over the more urgent.

I would encourage every disciple to find ways to be involved in the most important work going. I don't think anyone is going to blast you if you don't, but you will discover so many blessings if you will. You will never find greater satisfaction than what you will experience when you know you have had a part in pointing someone to Heaven. Redirecting people away from the disastrous path they may now be taking to put them on the road to Heaven is worth making some adjustments. It might be beneficial to us and to others to take a second look at how we have lined up our priorities.

DON'T UNDERESTIMATE SATAN

Knowing there were several evangelistic contacts I needed to make, I found myself driving around town making one inconsequential stop after another. It was almost as if I was looking for reasons that day to dodge the work I valued most. Then it dawned on me, *just one of the ways Satan works to keep me from my most significant duty.* The last thing Satan wants is for anyone to give their life to Christ.

Paul wrote to the Thessalonians, "For we wanted to come to you-certainly I, Paul, did again and again-but Satan blocked our way" (1 Thessalonians 2:18). Paul wanted to come to them and such a visit, no doubt, would have been beneficial to him and the Christians in that city. But Satan, knowing that, was successful in keeping Paul away. Satan has great power and he will use it to hinder the real work we set out to do for the Lord. He doesn't want us to help anyone know the Lord.

Matthew 13 records that Jesus told a parable, "The kingdom of heaven is like a man who sowed good seed in his field. But while everyone was sleeping, his enemy came and sowed weeds among the wheat, and went away. When the wheat sprouted and formed heads, then the weeds also appeared. The owner's servants came to him and said, 'Sir, didn't you sow good seed in your field? Where then did the weeds come from?' "An enemy did this,' he replied..." (Matthew 13: 24-28).

We can expect the enemy to hinder us from planting the seed. We can expect him to pollute the seed or do anything else he can do to keep the gospel seed from taking root in a person's heart. The point is that we need to stay alert through every step of the evangelistic process, knowing that by our effort, we are making Satan about as angry as he gets. He will not fall over and play dead. He will not give up easy. We find our strength and ultimate victory in those wonderful words found in 1 John 4:4, "You, dear children, are from God and have overcome them, because the one who is in you is greater than the one who is in the world." The successful soul-winner is the one who by the power of the Lord keeps on keeping on even in the face of the enemy's best effort.

BE UNITED

Nothing hinders our work for the Lord more than disharmony. Our best work is done by joining hands in a united effort. So much more can be achieved by multiple people than one or two people trying to do the job. Not only that, but we gain credibility when the world sees a people united. That is probably what Jesus had in mind when, after praying for the apostles, He prayed about the unity of all believers in John 17:20-23: "My prayer is not for them alone. I pray also for those who will believe in me through their message, that all of them may be one, Father, just as you are in me and I in you. May they also be in us so that the world may believe that you have sent me. I have given them the glory that you gave me, that they may be one as we are one: I in them and you in me – so that they may be brought to complete unity. Then the world will know that you sent me and have loved them even as you have loved me."

How can we effectively present the gospel when we, the Lord's people, are fighting over what the message should be. We have opposing views about the methods that should be used. We may even fight over whether evangelism has a place in the work of the church and if so, where should it be placed among our priorities. Evangelism, like so many areas of church work is greatly hindered by the disharmony of God's people.

It has been years since I heard the story, so details may not be exactly right. I understand it happened seventy-five or a hundred years ago in Kansas. A pre-school child, a beautiful little girl, was lost late one day. Evidently, she had wandered into one of the large wheat fields and could not find her way out. People gathered quickly to search. Many neighbors came in their wagons and their vehicles from miles around. They scattered through the fields. It was getting dark and still no little girl. Finally, one of the men said, "You know, we have enough people here that if we were to join hands, we could cover every inch of these fields in no time at all. If she is here, we could not help but find her. Quickly they were instructed to join hands and move across the first field. The line was so long that the person farthest south would have a hard time hearing the call of the one placed farthest north. In less than twenty minutes, someone from the middle of the long line cried out, "Here she is, we've found her." The mother and father, naturally, ran as fast as they could to the place from where they heard the voice. But, oh, how their hearts were broken when they saw the scene before them. That precious little girl had been bitten by a rattlesnake and her lifeless body was lying on the ground with her little doll held closely to her chest. The mother dropped to the ground. Lifting the little girl, who had been the apple of her eye, into her arms, she began to sob over and over, "if only we had joined hands earlier. Why didn't we join hands earlier?"

When I consider all those beautiful people who are going out into eternity without the Lord, I am compelled to say, "if only we had joined hands earlier Why didn't we join hands earlier?"

EVANGELISM NEEDS TO BE MODELED

It has been my observation that almost always, those who become effective soul-winners are people who have seen evangelism modeled. Sometimes over and over they have observed someone in action. I once heard the late James Kennedy speak. He was the originator of the Coral Ridge Method that was called Evangelism Explosion. Some years back, it was all the rage among churches interested in evangelism. You might remember his presentation started with the question, "If you should meet Jesus and He asked you, why should I let you into my Heaven, how would you answer?" Many churches simply took Kennedy's plan almost word for word and used it just the way he published it. Others adapted it for their use by altering a few doctrinal points where they differed with him. But it was widely used, quite effectively, for a good number of years.

Kennedy told those of us in his audience that Evangelism Explosion wasn't really his brainchild. As a young preacher he traveled to a church where he had been asked to conduct an evangelistic meeting. Recounting his experience there, he said time after time he sat in various homes and other settings listening while the pastor used the same presentation over and over to bring people to Jesus. Kennedy shared with us that when he returned to Florida, having heard the presentation numerous times, he had committed it to memory and began to use it in his own visitation. He said he even slapped his leg at the same point in the presentation as did the gentleman from whom he learned. Thus, Evangelism Explosion was born because evangelism had been modeled for Kennedy.

Knowing how crucial seeing evangelism modeled is to the prospective soul-winner is just one of the reasons for us to take someone with us when we go out in our community to speak to people about Jesus. The best evangelistic programs for churches are those programs where the recruit gets to observe the experienced worker doing the work.

SALUTE THE VICTORYS

Being born again is the most important thing that happens to a person in this life because it opens a spot in heaven for that one who has been saved. One coming to know the Lord is a big deal. It's the biggest deal! It is recorded in Luke 15:10 that Jesus declared, "In the same way, I tell you, there is rejoicing in the presence of the angels of God over one sinner who repents." When one comes to the Lord, it's a big deal in Heaven and it ought to be a big deal in the church.

To make little of those who have make decisions for Jesus is to give the impression that nothing too important has happened, but the truth is the angels in heaven are singing. It's going to be hard to get anyone interested in doing evangelism if they have gotten the impression that it is of little consequence.

When, in our ministry, many people were coming to the Lord and being baptized at times other than church meeting times, we had them come to the front of the auditorium on a Sunday. They were introduced, welcomed, applauded and people knew that something important had happened. In fact, some people were so impressed that something significant had happened that they decided they wanted to be part of the process in the future. Let's never be guilty of stifling the churches evangelistic efforts by seeming to place little importance on the decisions being made for Christ.

FOR YOUR CONSIDERATION

1. Why do you suppose people sometimes have difficulty evangelizing close family members?

2. Can you recite four of the steps we can take to pray evangelistically?

3. Why is prayer important to evangelism?

4. How do you feel about the statement, "most of us find a way to do the things we really want to do?"

5. What factors should be considered when priorities are set?

6. Why is it important not to underestimate Satan as we evangelize?

7. What part does unity play in evangelism?

8. What do you think, why have we not joined hands earlier?

9. Why is the modeling portion of evangelistic training so important?

10. What is the significance of saluting evangelic victories?

PART TWO

A PRACTICAL MANUAL FOR
RETURNING TO NEW TESTAMENT
EVANGELISM

HOW TO TELL YOUR STORY IN THREE MINUTES

We used to call it, "giving your testimony." In more recent times, I have heard it referred to as "telling your story." Regardless of what we call it, it is a tool that disciples can use effectively in multiple situations to point the unbeliever in a spiritual direction. I recommend every Christian take time to put theirs on paper and memorize it. Then, recruit a friend with whom to practice before using it for the spiritual good of people confronted in everyday life. It doesn't have to be long. In fact, it is most usable when not of great length. For best results, it should be given in three to five minutes. It can be constructed from a three-point outline. (1) My life before I met Christ, (2) How I met Christ, and (3) My life since I met Christ. The samples that follow are given simply as a guide. The details of every testimony, though formed from the same outline, will vary.

SAMPLE #1

My life before I met Christ - "I grew up in a home with two younger sisters and a little brother. My father was an alcoholic. Fighting, sometimes physical, and constant bickering were regular occurrences in our home. Extreme poverty was one of the results. Because of his alcoholism, I don't remember my father holding a job for more than two weeks. We lived in rental house after rental house, always moving when the owner demanded the rent money. School was hard because of the constant moving and absences. Self-image became a real problem for me, resulting in an abnormally introverted personality. The only times of happiness I remember during my childhood were those times I lived for extended periods with my maternal grandparents. When I was approaching fifteen years of age, I returned from a lengthy time of residing with grandparents to live with my parents and siblings. They had settled in a four-room house that was owned by a family member who provided the house out of pity for us. Those were often difficult times, but I stayed there through my high school years."

How I came to know Christ – "When I came back home to live in my early teen years, three things happened that helped guide me to a safe and, ultimately, delightful future. First, I got involved and eventually excelled in sports. That was important because it kept me in school. The second and third occurrences were even more significant. Through a friend by the name of Joe, I found a church. Joe's friendship and the encouragement of the youth group helped to keep me afloat. The third factor was that George, the young preacher, took me under his wing, and I think made me his special project. He often discreetly spoke to me about spiritual matters and particularly the advantages of one having Christ in his life, but most of all he was a friend to me. Due to that kind of positive influence and the life modeling of my new friends, a wonderful thing happened one Sunday night. When the decision song was being sung, I fought back the feelings brought on by my bashfulness. I remember saying to myself, *I can do this! Jesus died for me, I need to step out and live for Him.* I accepted Jesus, being baptized the same hour."

My life since I met Christ – "Oh, how that Sunday night decision changed my life. I can't tell you that I've had no problems since that time. The fact is, I've had many, but that's okay because since then, I've had a power beyond myself to deal with whatever comes my way. I've not had to tackle life on my own. It was in the youth group of that church, while still in high school that I discovered a young lady with whom I became infatuated. Eventually, we fell in love and were married. We have lived our lives together as husband and wife, parents, grandparents, co-servants, co-authors and best friends. One of the grandest things Jesus did for me was to give me that home I never had as a child. Beyond that, I've lived with real purpose and known the joy of being a servant on his way to heaven. You see, Christ turned my life around, taking it from bad to something special. I want you to know that He can do for you everything he's done for me."

SAMPLE #2

Sample number two is for those people who sometimes tell me, "I don't really have a testimony because I grew up in a Christian home and became a Christian early. I don't know what it is like to live life without Christ." When all is said and done, that person has the greatest testimony of all. His or her story might go like this:

My life before I met Christ – "I grew up in a home with wonderful parents who loved me very much. My brother is two years older than me. Life was always pretty normal. I received spiritual instruction at home and was taken just about every Sunday to a special church where I heard Christ talked about in class and then from the pulpit. Many of my activities revolved around the church. Most of my best friends were there, and we went to summer church camp together several times. It was, for me, a normal part of life. I was aware of people who from time to time were accepting the Lord. Sometimes it was older children or youth who were being baptized on Sundays. Sometimes it was adults. For almost as far back as I can remember, I think I knew that someday I would want to give my life to Jesus."

How I met Christ – "Then one day Emily, my best friend, told me she had talked with the preacher about becoming a Christian. She was to be baptized at the end of the church service the following Sunday. I thought about what Emily had told me for a while. Before the end of the week I went to my parents and told them about Emily and informed them I thought it was time I gave my life to Jesus as well. They were thrilled and told me they had been praying for that to someday happen ever since I had come into the world. They wanted to make sure I understood what I was doing. They didn't want me to become a Christian for no other reason than that Emily was doing it. So, they called the preacher. He came by and read some scripture to me, so I would understand the commitment I was making. On Sunday Emily and I, and two of our other friends were baptized. As the preacher said, it was the second time I was born."

My life since I met Christ – "That might sound rather routine to you, but I want you to know there was nothing routine about it. My life has not been the same since I gave it to Christ. I had a good life before, but not one with direction, purpose, and power like I have now. Jesus has given me that. I have looked to Him when making life's decisions, and He has never let me down. I have a wonderful Christian husband and two children we are raising to someday walk with Him. I can't imagine life without Jesus. Time and time again when I've been going through something difficult, I've prayed to Him, knowing that He would see me through. Life is so much more comforting when you know you are on your way to Heaven. That is what Jesus has done for me, and He can do it for you as well."

SAMPLE #3

Because we want everyone to have a sample testimony from which they can work, let's consider one more.

My life before I met Christ – "I was in my mid-thirties. We had recently moved to Atlanta from another part of the country. The children were still in diapers, and the wife was unhappy with our new surroundings. Things just were not good, and I feared we were not going to make it as a family. As unhappy as I was, that was not what I wanted. Religion had been part of both my life and my wife's life, but not a very big part. At that time, both of us would have told you we were Christians, but we weren't. We were occasional churchgoers who had never made any real commitment to the Lord. I had just boarded a plane from Washington headed home to Atlanta from a business trip, and I guess I was at just about my lowest point. I knew something had to change, but I didn't know how I could make that happen."

How I came to know Christ – "After I sat down in the window seat, a gentleman, perhaps a couple of years older than me, sat down beside me in the aisle seat. As he did so, he smiled and extended a hand to me saying, "I'm Jerry." I introduced myself, and then settled in my seat for the take off. When we were in the air, he opened his brief case and took out a Bible which he started silently reading. After a couple of minutes, maybe because I was looking for some answers, I asked him with a little uncomfortable giggle, 'find anything helpful in there?' He answered by sort of thumping his Bible and saying, 'Everything in here is helpful.' We talked and he told me how Jesus was making a real difference in his life. After we landed, he told me about his church and suggested that Sunday I bring the wife and children there to see what was going on. I told him I would, and I did. Less than a month later, both my wife and I had made decisions to accept Jesus, and it's been all uphill ever since."

My life since I met Christ – "That was almost twenty years ago, and oh how our lives have changed. I've never seen my wife happier. Instead of being a struggle, life is an adventure every day. Our two children are now young adults, with one in Bible college and the other happily serving the Lord. The Lord has been good to us in every way. It's not that we get everything we want or that life always swings the way we want it to. But even when there are struggles, the Lord shows the way and provides the wherewithal to keep things under control. He is the source we turn to for the real needs in our lives, and He never lets us down. You need to know that if you are willing to give your life to Him, He'll never let you down either. I highly recommend Him to you. You can't go wrong with Jesus."

CIRCUMSTANCES IN WHICH YOU CAN USE YOUR STORY

I am sure you'll come up with many circumstances in which you will be able to use your story. Here are a few suggestions to get you started:

1. We can use our testimony on those occasions when attempting to minister to a person in trouble.
2. A good time to share your story is when someone tells you of their unhappiness.
3. One searching for meaning in life needs to hear about what Jesus has done for you.
4. A person who speaks to you about his/her disillusionment with religion should be told what Christ can do with a life.
5. Someone who feels no one cares about him/her can find assurance by hearing what Jesus did for you.
6. Share your testimony with that new friend as you are getting to know one another.
7. Tell your story to that person who is out to get all he can out of life.
8. Our testimony can be used when we approach a person to stir spiritual interest in his/her heart.
9. We can tell our story to that friend as we converse in general conversation.

10. We can share our story when we are asked why religion is so important to us.

YOUR ASSIGNMENT!

Please take some time to write your story by filling out the three main points below:

1. I. MY LIFE BEFORE I MET CHRIST!

2. II. HOW I MET CHRIST!

3. III. MY LIFE SINCE I MET CHRIST!

CHAPTER 9

A PRESENTATION FOR LEADING ONE TO JESUS

Well here it is! Several times I've mentioned a presentation I put together as a twenty-three-year-old, allowing me to have something to say when confronting the one who is outside the Lord. I make no claim to it being the best thing since sliced bread. I don't even suggest it is among the better scripted presentations you might choose. All I can say in its favor is, it's a method that makes use of scripture that's worked for me for almost fifty years. Hundreds have accepted Jesus after hearing this simple presentation. Perhaps if I had put it aside at some point for something more sophisticated or complete, more people would have been won. I don't know.

I have often heard the use of scripted presentations criticized, and, perhaps, that criticism is valid. I just know that, in my case, I needed something stored away in my mind to have the courage to do such work. I had to know I had something to say. I guess, I desperately needed it in the beginning and never found a reason to abandon it as the years passed and some continued to come to Christ.

I was once leading a seminar in northeast Indiana in which I was teaching this presentation to twenty or twenty-five folks. It was a three-night event. On the second night, as I got into the meat of the actual presentation, one of the students kept making remarks like, "This wouldn't work with my husband. My husband wouldn't respond to this in a million years. Good luck in getting my husband to listen to this."

After the seminar session that evening, I asked the host preacher of that little church about the husband who was referenced several times that night. He told me, "He's a good man who comes to church with his family often. He's been doing that for almost ten years but has never accepted the Lord."

"Will he get home from work in time for us to visit with him before the final seminar session tomorrow evening?" I asked.

"I think so," the preacher told me. The wife was shocked to see us when we showed up; at her house the following evening around five o'clock. A few minutes later I got to meet her husband who didn't seem like the hardcase his wife had implied he was.

"Ed, could we talk seriously for a few minutes?" I asked after we had gotten acquainted. He gave his permission. I opened my Bible and began to share what I had been teaching in the seminar. He paid close attention and seemed to respond well. Twenty-five minutes later, I asked, "Ed, don't you think it's about time for you to make that decision to accept Jesus?"

The silence that followed seemed to last for five minutes but was probably not more than a minute or two. I gave him the opportunity to ponder my question as he looked at the floor. Finally, he looked up and said, "Yes, I think it is." There was rejoicing in that house that evening as we prayed, giving thanks for Ed's decision. We made plans for his baptism on Sunday. As I look back on Ed's situation, I believe he probably had never become a Christian simply because no one had ever asked him to.

That evening, the wife who had been so skeptical the previous evening, remarked to the attendees, "It works, I can assure you, firsthand, that it really does work." We will first examine the outline before looking at my version pretty much word for word. I would suggest you can make the adjustments you feel are appropriate for you or put together your own presentation from

scratch. But regardless, give yourself the best chance for help-
ing someone get to Heaven by preparing appropriately in some
way for the big opportunity. To use this approach, learn the outline. Become thoroughly acquainted with the scriptures. After
you have committed the outline to memory, read the script over
and over until you see how it logically falls together. Perhaps, I
need to offer this alert. I put this together several decades back.
A lot of water has gone under the bridge since then. I honestly do
not remember if I borrowed from the work of others in putting
it together. I certainly would acknowledge that person or those
people and express my deepest gratitude if there are such people.

AN OUTLINE FOR USE IN LEADING ONE TO JESUS

1. One must be shown why he/she needs the Lord.
    a. All have sinned. Romans 3:23
    b. The wages of sin is death (separation). Romans 6:23a
    c. The answer to the sin problem is Jesus. Romans 6:23b
       and John 3:16
2. One must be shown how to accept the free gift. Acts 8:26-
   39, Acts 2:38, Acts 16:31, and Romans 10:9
    a. Faith Act 8:37a and Acts 16:31
    b. Repent. Acts 2:38
    c. Confess Acts 8:37b and Romans 10:9
    d. Be Baptized Acts 8:38 and Acts 2:38
3. Ask for a decision.
4. Deal with Satan's objections and if appropriate ask again
   for a decision.

A PRESENTATION FOR LEADING ONE TO THE LORD

"Ray, it has been good to get acquainted with you and your
family recently. I sort of feel obligated to tell you that the most

important thing in my life is my relationship with Jesus. Could I take a few minutes to tell you about that?"

WHY WE NEED JESUS:

"Let me read you a verse from Romans 3:23, God tells us something very important there. It says, 'For all have sinned and fall short of the glory of God." Ray, I think most of us have a pretty good idea about what sin is. It is literally missing the mark. God, our creator, has set standards for us. When we fall short of those standards, we have sinned. Now, there are two ways to miss the mark. We can miss the mark by doing what God has revealed in His Word we are not to do. I bet you can think of what some of those things are, can't you, Ray..?"

"But there is another way we can sin. It is by doing absolutely nothing at all. You see, God has instructed us to do certain things with our lives. When we don't do those, we miss the mark and commit sin."

"Exactly three chapters over, in Romans 6:23, it tells us something else about sin, 'For the wages of sin is death, but the gift of God is eternal life in Christ Jesus our Lord.' The word *wages* is an interesting word, as used here. We know that when we work our job, we receive wages for that work. It is the result of our work. The Bible is saying that the result of sin is death. Now Ray, I want you to think of death as separation from God. Missing the mark or sinning separates us from God. God is holy. He is without sin and He will not allow Himself to be where sin is present."

"But praise be to God, Ray, there is some good news in the latter part of Romans 6:23. It says, '...but the gift of God is eternal life in Christ Jesus our Lord.' John 3:16 says, 'For God so loved the world that he gave his one and only Son, that whoever believes in him shall not perish but have eternal life.' God loved us so much that he didn't want to remain separated from us, so he sent his Son, Jesus, into the world to live a life without sin. As one who was sinless, He could then take our punishment for us. You remember that punishment is death, so Jesus died for us on a cross as punishment for our sins. He is the only one who could do that, because He is the only person to ever live a life totally without sin. There was no one else qualified to be our sacrifice. So, it tells us in the last part of John 3:16 that, 'whoever believes in Him shall not perish, but have eternal life.'

"Ray, let me go back and briefly summarize what I have said so far. All of us have sinned. The presence of that sin separates us from God. God loved us so much, He could not stand to be parted from us. So, He sent Jesus into the world. Jesus lived a sinless life, making Him eligible to die for our sins, which He did. Those who accept his gift of forgiveness by embracing Him will then, as disciples forgiven of our sins, be with God in Heaven for eternity. It's pretty easy to see why we need Jesus, isn't it, Ray?"

"I'm sure you noticed in Romans 6:23 that it refers to our forgiveness as a *gift* from Jesus. Salvation or forgiveness is a free gift from God through Jesus. What must one do to receive a free gift? If I had a ten-dollar bill in my hand and held it out to you and said, 'Ray, I want you to have this gift.' What would be required for you to have it? That's right. You would have to receive it. The same is true of the Lord's gift of salvation to us. He does not force it on us. We cannot buy it or earn it, but we must receive it."

HOW WE ACCEPT THE FREE GIFT:

"Now, I want to take you to an example we find in the Bible of a man receiving the gift of salvation. It's in Acts 8:26-39. Listen as I read:

'Now an angel of the Lord said to Philip, go south on the road - the desert road – that goes down from Jerusalem to Gaza. So he started out, and on the way he met an Ethiopian eunuch, an important official in charge of all the treasure of the Kandake (which means 'Queen of the Ethiopians'). This man had come to Jerusalem to worship, and on his way home was sitting in his chariot reading the Book of Isaiah the prophet. The Spirit told Philip, go to that chariot and stay near it.'

'Then Philip ran up to the chariot and heard the man reading Isaiah the prophet, 'Do you understand what you are reading?' Philip asked.'

'How can I," he said,' unless someone explains it to me?' So he invited Philip to come up and sit with him.'

"This is the passage of Scripture the eunuch was reading:

'He was led like a sheep to the slaughter, and as a lamp before its shearer is silent, so he did not open his mouth. In his humiliation he was deprived of justice. Who can speak of his descendants? For his life was taken from the earth.'

The eunuch asked Philip, 'Tell me, please, who is the prophet talking about, himself or someone else?' Then Philip began with that very passage of Scripture and told him the good news about Jesus.

'As they traveled along the road, they came to some water and the eunuch said, 'Look, here is water. What can stand in the way of my being baptized?' Philip said, 'If you believe with all your heart, you may.' The eunuch answered, 'I believe that Jesus Christ is the Son of God. And he gave orders to stop the chariot. Then both Philip and the eunuch went down into the water and Philip baptized him. When they came up out of the water, the Spirit of the Lord suddenly took Philip away, and the eunuch did not see him again, but went on his way rejoicing.'

"So, Philip was led to a place where he found a man, an important man who was treasurer to a queen reading from Old Testament Scripture. Obviously, he was a believer in the true God, for not only was he reading from the Bible, but had been to Jerusalem to worship. While he knew about God, he knew nothing of Jesus. It so happened that he was reading from what we know as the fifty-third chapter of Isaiah which foretold the crucifixion of Jesus. Philip was invited up into the chariot and beginning with that Scripture told the Ethiopian about Jesus. Evidently, he was excited when he heard, because when they came to some water, he said, 'Look, here is water. Why can't I be baptized?' We then see Philip's answer in a footnote at the bottom of the page where he is basically saying, 'Let's get first things first. You can be baptized if you believe with all your heart. That is *faith*, Ray – believing in Jesus with all your heart, and it is our first step to receiving the gift of salvation. In Acts 8:31, the Philippian jailer was told, '...Believe in the Lord Jesus Christ and you will be saved...' Believe in Jesus with all your heart! One cannot be saved without that kind of faith. Faith in Jesus is where it starts for us."

"The second step is not spelled out in this account, so I am quickly turning to Acts 2:37-38, so we can clearly see and understand it. 'When the people heard this, they were cut to the heart and said to Peter and the other apostles, 'Brothers, what shall we do?' Peter replied, 'Repent and be baptized every one of you in the name of Jesus Christ for the forgiveness of your sins. And you will receive the gift of the Holy Spirit.'"

"Did you notice, Ray, that Peter said we are to *repent?* That is step two – repent. I guess that is one of those religious words we throw around, but really all it means is to be sorry for our sins — so sorry that we are willing to turn away from them. We cannot receive this gift without repentance."

"You remember in verse three of Acts eight that the eunuch said, 'I believe that Jesus Christ is the Son of God.' That is what we sometimes call the good confession. And that is the third step in receiving the free gift of salvation. We are to *confess* or state to others what we believe about Jesus. Romans 10:9 says, 'if you declare with your mouth, Jesus is Lord,' and believe in your heart that God raised him from the dead, you will be saved.'

There is one more thing I want to point out, Ray. In the account of Philip and the Ethiopian in verse thirty-eight, it's recorded, 'And he gave the orders to stop the chariot. Then both

Philip and the eunuch went down into the water and Philip baptized him.'

'He *baptized* him.' You will remember a moment ago we read
from Acts 2:38 where Peter instructed, 'Repent and be baptized
every one of you in the name of Jesus Christ for the forgiveness
of your sins. And you will receive the gift of the Holy Spirit. That
is exactly what the eunuch was doing. He was being baptized in
the name of Jesus."

ASK FOR A DECISION:

"We have talked about four ways that Ethiopian reacted to
Jesus as he was offered that free gift: First, he had faith or believed with all his heart. Second — though it's not spelled out
here as it is in other conversion accounts — He, no doubt, repented. He was so sorry for his sins that he turned from them.
Third, he confessed that Jesus is the Son of God. The fourth thing
we see demonstrated is his baptism in the name of the Lord Jesus
Christ. Four simple logical reactions when he heard about Jesus
and what Jesus did for Him. Ray, just as surely as Jesus died for
that Ethiopian, he died for you. Are you ready to respond as did
he? Are you ready to make your decision to accept Jesus?

DEAL WITH SATAN'S OBJECTION AND, IF APPROPRIATE,
ASK AGAIN FOR A DECISION.

Satan does not give up easy. It's not unusual for him to plant
some excuse in the mind of the prospect for not making that decision for the Lord. I don't like to give up easy either. I normally
take a little time to speak to that person about the obstacle without being pushy, and if that one seems to come around, I will
once again ask for a decision. Example Below.

Prospect – "It all sounds good, but there are some things in my life that I need to work through before I can totally commit my life to Jesus."

Interviewer – "I understand your reluctance, and I appreciate that when you make that decision, you want it to be the real thing. Let me point out something that we didn't talk about when we looked at Acts 2:38. 'Peter replied, Repent and be baptized, every one of you, in the name of Jesus Christ for the forgiveness of your sins. And you will receive the gift of the Holy Spirit.'

"Did you catch that last line? 'You will receive the gift of the Holy Spirit.' You know what that means, Ray? It means that when we become Christians, God, in the form of his Holy Spirit, comes to live in us. The fact is, we have power after receiving Jesus that we did not have before. I'm suggesting that if you wait until you can conquer, on your own, whatever you are struggling with, you will probably never get there. The best way for you to approach it may be to accept Jesus, receiving power you did not have before. With the power of the Holy Spirit then, you can conquer your demons. It could be a disaster for you to wait until you get it all under control on your own. Let Jesus empower you to do that. Don't you think you ought to go ahead and give your life to Jesus?"

YOUR ASSIGNMENT

After spending some time studying and memorizing the outline for the presentation, write from memory the main points and sub-points with Scripture below.

CHAPTER 10

WHEN THE ANSWSER IS "NO"

I have spent the last few years of my life primarily as a writer. Early on, I received helpful counsel from experienced writers who told me, "If you're going to be a writer, you need to brace yourself for a lot of rejection." They were right. Most writers, even the super successful ones, will tell you their work was rejected regularly before they got a foothold in the industry. A writer unwilling to put up with rejection will probably never make it as a writer. Rejection is part of the success process.

I always have been quick to tell evangelistic workers the same. You can expect your message of love to be rejected far more than it will be received. But, like the writer, we must be ready to withstand the negative responses for there to be any success. I kept no records on such things, but my guess is that through the years, I probably got a positive response about one out of every seven or eight times I made a gospel presentation. At times, the percentages were better and at other times even worse. For the sake of souls, we must not become discouraged. People need the Lord, and most will never receive Him unless they are confronted by someone who cares. My advice for those times when *no* is the answer is that we keep the door open. I can think of numerous times when a person was ultimately won to the Lord after I politely walked away, only later to find my way back through that door that had been left open.

Sometimes we may not succeed because we take *no* as a person's final answer when we have asked him to accept the Lord. It could be that we only need to help him past one obstacle that Satan has put in his mind. Let me share with you some of the obstacles I have heard most frequently and how we might deal with them. Please don't feel that by taking it a step further, you are trying to push the person into something they don't want. I'm not interested in pushing anyone into anything, but I also want to give my best effort since a soul is at stake.

I suspect today's culture provides some stumbling blocks you will not find here, but if we can get a hold on those below, it shouldn't be hard for us to figure out how to deal with the rest.

I INTEND TO SOME DAY

You make your presentation before asking, "Don't you think it's time for you to receive the Lord? "

Your friend who has been intently listening for the past half hour responds, "It all sounds good. I intend to do it someday, but now is not the time." How do we respond. I've heard this from time to time through the years, and I have usually responded with something like this:

"If you intend to do it someday, then you obviously believe it's the right thing to do. If it is right, then it is wrong to put it off. Have you ever considered what you are losing by putting it off? Every day you wait is another day of blessings you have forfeited. Not only that, but we don't know when the Lord will return, or our lives will end. Waiting is like playing Russian roulette with our souls. Satan knows how to play us, and he knows that if he can keep us believing long enough that there is no urgency, he's got us exactly where he wants us. Someone once correctly said, "The road to hell is paved with good intentions." It's your decision, and I don't want to try to push you into doing what you don't want to do, but it's my concern for you that compels me to ask again, Don't you want to go ahead and make that most important decision of your life?

I'M NOT GOOD ENOUGH

You talk with one about his decision for the Lord and then ask, "Are you ready to accept Jesus?"

He pauses for a minute or two before telling you, "I understand pretty much everything you said, but I'm not good enough to be a Christian." What would you tell him? Here's something to get you started.

"You know…the fact we are not good enough is the very reason that Jesus died as a sacrifice on that cross for us. Any goodness or righteousness I have, is because Jesus shed his blood on the cross to take away my sins. He's done the same for you, and there is no sin too big for his blood to cover. It is because of our sin or badness that we need Jesus. You'll remember that earlier we talked about repentance and said it is being so sorry for our sin that we are ready to not only acknowledge it but turn away from it. When we receive Jesus, it is as if we have never sinned. All you must do to be totally sinless is to receive Jesus as your Lord and Savior. It doesn't matter how bad we might have been in the past. Are you ready to do that?"

I HAVE NEVER MARRIED THE ONE WITH WHOM I'M LIVING

You visit with a couple who have been in worship at your church for four or five recent Lord's days. They are so cordial and receptive that you decide to share with them the good news about Jesus. At the conclusion of your presentation, you suggest to them, "Don't you think the two of you ought to give your lives to Jesus?"

The gentleman responds, "It all sounds good. I've thought about it for a long time, but there is something you need to know about us. We have been living together for almost three years, but we've never been married. Wouldn't that disqualify us from becoming Christians?" In today's world we need to be ready to answer that question. Here is how I have responded.

"Obviously, you understand that to live together outside of marriage is unacceptable to God, and therefore sin. You would not have asked that question if you did not recognize that. But to answer your question, no, it does not disqualify you from being a Christian. We need Jesus because of our past sin. We talked about repentance earlier. The question is, are you ready to repent of that sin? Such repentance would include setting things right, being sorry, and turning away from that sin. We can arrange to put things in order this very night if you are ready to give your life to Him. It's all about his forgiveness. He wants to forgive you if you are ready to embrace Him. Remember, there is not one of us who came into the Lord without sin in our past."

I DON'T KNOW ENOUGH

After sharing with the potential Christian, he tells you, "Sounds good, but I just don't know enough to make a decision like that." My response to that would be simple.

"I knew very little when I became a Christian and here I am today, sharing the Bible with you. There is a lot to learn and hopefully I will be learning for the rest of my life, but the only things you need to know in order to receive Christ and obtain his forgiveness are the things we talked about tonight. We need to know that we are sinners, separated from God by our sin and that Jesus is the solution to the sin problem. We need to know that by receiving his gift of salvation, we are forgiven and are united with God. We need to know that by virtue of that decision, we become his servants. We need to know that we want what Jesus offers. Do you want that?"

YOU AREN'T INTERESTED IN ME, I'M GAY

You are in a seat on a bus or train that takes you to work in the city. You are reading your Bible. That sparks a conversation with a young man about things spiritual. You talk with him about Jesus. Eventually, you ask, "Don't you think you would like to receive the forgiveness Jesus offers?

The young man comes back with, "If you knew who I am, you wouldn't be interested in me, I'm gay and have for a time been living a gay lifestyle." Does that end your conversation? It shouldn't. Here is a suggestion for the direction you might take.

"Because you are gay doesn't mean I am not interested in you. God loves you, and so do I. We have people in our church who once lived the gay lifestyle. Yes, you are right in assuming that God disapproves of such a lifestyle (I would not try to do any biblical teaching until I built a relationship that would support such an open discussion). But it is not an unforgiveable sin when true repentance occurs. And I don't want you to tell me that once a person enters that kind of lifestyle, he/she cannot go back. I know better. I am aware of several people who have done just that. And I believe with God's help, you can do the same thing."

I'M AFRAID I WON'T BE ABLE TO STAY WITH IT

Many people have observed that others who have become Christians have failed. They see people live only half-heartedly for Jesus, and they don't want to start until they know they can stay with it. So, when asked to receive Christ, they may respond with, "Not now, I'm afraid I won't be able to stay with it."

I usually respond to that one and those sounding a lot like it with, "You are absolutely right in thinking you can't live the

Christian life on your own. But thanks be to God, we don't have to accomplish that with only our own strength. Do you remember what we read in Acts 2:38? It tells us in that verse that when we accept Christ, God's Holy Spirit comes to live in us. That gives us power beyond ourselves to use in becoming what God wants us to be. It's true that many people do fail in the Christian life, but we don't have to. A Christian life that will bring joy to anyone can be sustained when one allows the Holy Spirit to do his work. The Christian life would be impossible for us left to our own ability. That is why God implanted his power within us. When you accept Christ, you will accept the resource that will help you stay faithful when you are willing to apply yourself."

I AM WAITING ON MY HUSBAND (WIFE)

Sometimes one who has been asked to accept Jesus might respond with, "I plan to become a Christian, but for now I'm waiting on my husband (wife)." My response:

"It would please me greatly, should both of you become Christians at the same time. A home centered in Christ Jesus is a beautiful thing. But the reality is that salvation is a personal matter and should not depend on what another person does or doesn't do. He may be waiting on you. By your making your decision to trust Jesus, he may be led to do the same. You have a wonderful family. Even if your husband doesn't become a Christian now, it is better for your children to have one Christian parent than none at all. We need to do what we know to do, and then help those we love to do what they need to do. Satan is having his way when we delay our decision for Jesus for any reason. Don't you think you ought to go ahead and do what you know is right?"

I CAN'T ATTEND CHURCH REGULARLY

The person who has heard the gospel presentation listens intently. The evangelist asks, "Will you receive the Lord?" He responds by stating, "You sure paint a rosy picture, and I would love to be a Christian, but it's impossible for me to attend church on Sunday."

We might answer with, "Well, we won't go into it now, but church attendance is important. Hebrews 10:25 tells us not to give up meeting together. However, we are talking about your personal salvation here. We are talking about allowing Jesus to cleanse you of your sins that you can be one with him and someday be in Heaven. That is what is most important. If Sunday morning work is the problem, there are times other than Sunday mornings when we meet. You can take advantage of those until your situation changes. If you don't have transportation, we can take care of that immediately. Make your decision to follow Jesus, and we can work through any obstacles you may have to face to be faithful to him. Will you do that?"

I'M WAITING FOR THAT FEELING

There are still some people who believe that when they are *chosen* for salvation, a certain feeling will come over them. I hear it less these days, but in the past when it was offered to me as a reason for postponing one's acceptance of Jesus, I usually responded as follows:

"I know you agree with me that the Bible is God's Word and our guide in all things. I find nowhere in the Bible where we are taught that we are to wait for a certain feeling which will alert us that it is time to receive the Lord. There is no question that certain feelings are likely to be stirred up after one decides for Christ. When I gave my life to the Lord, there was great relief as if a weight had been lifted from my heart. There was joy and a feeling that I had just taken care of the most critical decision I would ever face. But the feeling came after I received Jesus. A feeling does not trigger one's response to the Lord. It is an awareness of our need for him that does that. The question is, do you realize why you need Jesus, and if so, are you ready to receive him?"

THEY FORCED ME TO GO TO CHURCH WHEN I WAS YOUNG

Let me suggest one more. That should give us a pretty good idea of how to handle Satan in these matters. You've made your presentation and asked, "Will you receive the Lord?"

The prospect answered, "I don't think so. They made me go to church when I was young, and I'm sort of glad to be away from all that for now."

I would respond something like this, "We're not talking about church attendance. I think if you would give your life to the Lord, you would see the value of being in church. I suspect you were forced many times to eat, but you didn't stop eating. No doubt, you were forced to sleep, but I dare say you are still sleeping most nights. I suspect your parents required you to go to church because they loved you and wanted what was best for you. You are an adult today and should be able to recognize for yourself what is good for you. The thing most needful for you now is forgiveness of your sins. Jesus did that for me, and He can do it for you if you are willing. Are you ready to receive him?"

YOUR ASSIGNMENT

Write in the space after each answer below, how you would respond:

1. "I want to think it over."

2. "I'm a good person. I don't need to do anything else."

3. "I need Sundays to rest."

CHAPTER 11

WHERE TO FIND THEM

S o, where do we find these people with whom we will share Christ? The Bible gives us some help with that.

THEY CAN BE FOUND IN CHURCH

In Acts 17:16-17 it is recorded that, "While Paul was waiting for them in Athens, he was greatly distressed to see that the city was full of idols. So he reasoned in the synagogue with both Jews and God-fearing Greeks..."

Paul had a starting point from which to share the gospel with these people. While they did not know Christ, they were acquainted with God, the Father. They were only a step away. I have found, through the years, that the people I can have the most success leading to the Lord are usually people I have become aware of through their attendance at church services. Sometimes they have only visited a few times. Others have been there for many years, yet, for whatever reason, have never trusted Jesus.

Why are they the best prospects? Because, by their attendance, they are demonstrating that they are interested. Also, often, by virtue of being in church, they have heard much that would likely bring them closer to a decision. Being already interested and acquainted with us, we do not have to work so hard to win their trust to earn the right to speak to them about such personal matters.

There is another factor to be taken into consideration as we consider the prospects we might find in our churches. Billy Graham once said, "The American church is one of the greatest mission fields in the world." I think he was saying that many who attend our churches Sunday after Sunday have never really been converted. They, too, need the Lord.

THEY MAY BE ASSOCIATED WITH THE BUSINESSES WE FREQUENT

Besides reasoning with those in the synagogues while waiting in Athens, Paul also taught day by day those in the marketplace (Acts 17:17). Let me first point out that we are usually constantly around the people with whom we work. It would be natural for us to look for ways to share Jesus with those co-workers who don't know him. An ideal situation for us to share our testimony.

Then there are those we see and greet often working in businesses we frequent. It may be the bank, the grocery store, the convenience store where we buy gas, or the waitress at the restaurant where we eat. No, there won't be time for us to share a lengthy spiritual message with them while they are on the job. But as we get to know that person, we might ask to take them out for a cup of coffee, or even invite him and his spouse to our home for a meal. And, of course, there will always be time to invite them to our church which can lead to other contact.

Here are some suggestions to increase our chances of successful encounters with those workers. No matter how our day has gone up to this time, we can smile at that person across the counter. Speak to them as we would to a friend. For years, I went into stores to pay for my gas and other purchases without saying a word. A few years back, due to circumstances I won't go into, I was reminded that this is a person taking my money. Now, I always find something positive to speak to him about and thank him for his help. Waitresses can be brutally abused. No Christian should ever be guilty of such a thing. I was once with a group of men who treated a waiter badly. He knew we were a Christian group. I tried to compensate for the actions of my friends, but I suspect that young man's mind and heart was, for a long time, closed to any testimony concerning Christ.

Another suggestion to enhance our ability to share with the businessperson is to pay our bills on time and be fair in all our controversial business dealings. A Christlike spirit opens doors to allow us to share, and it can increase the odds when we do.

THEY MAY BE FELLOW TRAVELERS

In chapter nine in which we introduced the gospel presentation, we learned of an Ethiopian Eunuch in Acts 8 who was traveling when he met Philip who gladly told him about Jesus.

The thing about much of our travel is that we are often seated next to a person, perhaps one we don't know, for a relatively long period of time. That can be a nuisance or an opportunity, depending on our mindset. The one who has a heart for evangelism will probably see the opportunity. It may be an opportunity with which he is not entirely comfortable, but, nevertheless, an opportunity. Recently, I heard my friend Roger, a strong Christian, tell how he happened to become a Christian. It all started for him when a gentleman he met while in flight witnessed to him about Jesus.

I remember a young man traveling to a foreign mission field where he was to serve for the summer. He told me about a man spilling his drink on him while they were boarded on an airliner. The young man said he arrived to be picked up by the missionaries smelling like liquor, but that was okay, because it opened a door for him to offer a testimony to a man who needed the Lord.

If we don't become so excited about the trip that we miss the open door, travel can offer us various openings for telling people about Jesus. That is bound to make the trip even better.

THEY MAY BE AT A SOCIAL GATHERING WE ATTEND

We are told that, "When one of the Pharisees invited Jesus to have dinner with him, he went to the Pharisee's house and reclined at the table. A woman in that town who lived a sinful life learned that Jesus was eating at the Pharisee's house, so she came there with an alabaster jar of perfume" (Luke 7:36-37). I won't take you through the whole account, but by the time we get to verse forty-eight, it is recorded, "Then Jesus said to her, 'Your sins are forgiven'."

So, here we see a story of a woman having her sins forgiven because Jesus was at a social event. I do not enjoy most social gatherings. That is probably why I've had little luck in evangelizing at such occasions. However, I've known a few who seemed to be masters in such venues. I have been more successful in a cozy dinner setting, perhaps involving two or three families.

One of the most successful pastors I have known tells me he was won to the Lord at a party where he would never had expected to even find a Christian. I suspect that pastor has been responsible for winning several hundred people to the Lord, while some of those reached have also won some. I guess we would have to say, it was a successful social event, at least for the cause of Christ.

SOME MIGHT BE FOUND INCARCERATED

The book of Acts, of course, gives us many reports of Jesus being shared. Chapter 16 mentions that after Paul and Silas had been stripped and beaten with rods before they were thrown into prison. They were put in the inner cell and their feet were fastened in stocks. Then, "About midnight Paul and Silas were praying and singing hymns to God, and the other prisoners were listening to them" (Acts 16:26).

Their witnessing was in the form of prayers and songs, but they found a way to get it done. Notice that it tells us the other prisoners were listening. You may know the rest of the story. Later these gentlemen had an opportunity to witness to the jailer. "...Believe in the Lord Jesus, and you will be saved – you and your household." Then they spoke the word of the Lord to him and to all others in his house. At that hour of the night, the jailer took them and washed their wounds; then immediately, he and all his household were baptized" (Acts 16:31-33).

I used to hear about churches and individuals who went into jails to minister and share the gospel message. Occasionally, in our time, I am made aware of organizations that have such ministries, but seldom do churches or individuals take it on themselves to do so. Where will we find a more spiritually-needy group? Could it be that we have tied our evangelistic efforts to building our local church? Jail evangelism may not help the local church grow much, but it surely has the potential to change some lives that need to be changed.

THEY CAN OFTEN BE FOUND IN THEIR OWN HOMES

When Paul called together the elders of the church at Ephesus, he, among other things, told them, "You know that I have not hesitated to preach anything that would be helpful to you but have taught you publicly and from house to house. I have declared to both Jews and Greeks that they must turn to God in repentance and have faith in our Lord Jesus" (Acts 20:20-21).

Paul was not speaking of *public house meetings* when he spoke of teaching them house-to-house. That is obvious because he reveals he taught them both *publicly* and *house-to-house*. I visualize Paul sitting down in the homes of these Ephesians one-on-one or one-to-family, sharing Jesus with them. Probably, at least half of those I have led to the Lord have been won with me sitting in a family room easy chair with a couple seated on the sofa or with me gathered with the family around the dining room table.

I admire those who are successfully using the *come and see method* of evangelism. I just want to see people embracing Christ, regardless of method. But I still believe the best method for the greatest number of churches in America continues to be home visitation. Dr. Orville Morgan was my professor of preaching in my college days. I remember well, him saying, "There is no excuse for neglecting home visitation." I think he was right. There is no doubt in my mind that visitation evangelism is still the best approach for most of us as we reach out to the lost. We get the opportunity to speak personally to people in an environment where they are most comfortable. It doesn't get better than that. Paul found it useful. I think those who commit to it today will continue to find it an enormous asset.

SOME WILL BE FOUND IN CHANCE MEETINGS

Mark reveals that, "Once again Jesus went out beside the lake. A large crowd came to him, and he began to teach them. As he walked along, he saw Levi son of Alphaeus sitting at the tax collector's booth. "Follow me," Jesus told him, and Levi got up and followed him."

It would seem that the calling to discipleship of Levi or Matthew as we often refer to him, was the result of a casual encounter – a chance meeting.

I have experienced that at times. A group of us were finishing the job of sealing our church parking lot late one day when an older couple drove up. Stopping short of where we had been working, they asked about the location of a different church where a seminar was being conducted. I told them where that church was located and invited them to come and visit with us some Sunday. To make a long story short, a while later, I had the opportunity to lead Mr. and Mrs. Reed to the Lord and baptize them. It happened quickly, and it happened because of a chance encounter. I have had opportunity to talk about Jesus to others I met by chance. Some of them were gloriously converted. These were people I met at softball games, committee meetings, luncheons, children's activities, the golf course, and other odd locations.

The point is that people who need Jesus can be found just about anywhere people go. It's really just a matter of identifying them and then finding or creating the right conditions for successfully sharing. That, of course, is not always easy, but because precious souls are at stake, it's worth the effort even when it's hard.

YOUR ASSIGNMENT

1. List three places where you might be able to find a person, who with some loving cultivation might be willing to hear what you have to say about Jesus.

2. Find someone with whom you will share your testimony this week, even if it is an immediate family member who already knows the Lord.

3. List three people who are part of your life, but do not know Jesus, for whom you will pray. Pray that you will soon have opportunity to speak to one of them about his/her need for Jesus.

CHAPTER 12

OLD IDEAS WITH POTENTIAL

Sometimes we may hang a piece of our out-of-date wardrobe in the closet with the idea, "I'll save it. It might become fashionable again." Occasionally we might discover that by making minor adjustments to that piece of clothing, it becomes useful again. The same principle can apply to evangelistic methods.

AN AMAZING OPPORTUNITY

I spent the last six years before I retired as preacher of my home church. It was a marvelous experience for me. I have often said since then that every preacher should have the opportunity to close out where he started. But there was something that happened in the last year or two before I retired that was for me mindboggling. To set the stage, let me tell you that as a young preacher, I, and two of the churches I served, had bus ministries. At one of those churches, we ran six bus routes each Sunday morning that brought more than two hundred children to our Sunday school and children's worship. Let me be quick to say that I am not advocating that we go out and buy a fleet of old school buses to bring back bus ministry. You may be aware of the reasons that make it almost impossible today. I'll not go into that.

We had a rather serious tornado in our town. We announced that our church building was open for anyone needing housing. A family with five children, ages from about six to sixteen, took

us up on our offer. After getting to know us, the children decided they would like to attend our Wednesday evening dinner
and children's program. The problem was they had no transportation. We had an old fifteen passenger van, we seldom used, I
asked one of our men to drive the van each Wednesday night to
pick up those children. An amazing thing happened. When I was
learning everything, one needed to know about bus ministry, I
was told, "You'll never put anyone on your bus if you don't go out
and find them. Then you must visit at their doors every Saturday."
That is how we did bus evangelism when I was a young man.

We picked up three or four additional children when the van
was taken to retrieve our tornado children the second week. The
next week there were more. Before long, our van driver was having to make a second trip to get all the children who wanted to
come. Then he was bringing in three loads. We purchased a second van and eventually replaced the old one with yet another.
Those two vans usually make two trips each. At times a third
trip has been required. We usually have the opportunity to feed
and teach thirty to fifty children on Wednesday nights that come
to us on our vans. There have been times when the number has
been in the seventies bracket. A few of those children have become Christians. Seed has been planted in the hearts of many.
Have we revived the old evangelistic bus ministry idea? Not really. The only similarity between what we are doing, and the bus
ministry idea is they both require vehicles. We have never once
gone to a home to ask if a child could join us on one of our vans.
We have done almost nothing the bus ministry "experts" insisted one must do to have a successful bus ministry. It just sort of
happened word of mouth. We believe God gave us this unlikely
ministry.

The point I am making is that many evangelistic ideas have
seemingly run their course. Most would need revamping to be
useful in our culture. But maybe we could take one or more of
those to adapt to our needs. Perhaps, we might see the potential

of some obsolete evangelistic tool that would serve us well if given new life through a new approach. Why not use your imagination and see what happens? Here are some old programs that might be useful with modification. Most of those mentioned below are for the church, but a couple are best utilized by the individual. I would love to hear from readers who have experienced successful innovations of old programs.

DISTRIBUTION OF LITERATURE

Some of us remember when distribution of gospel tracks was a common method used to get the gospel out to the lost. Often, they ended up in trash cans unread. I suspect most pieces went unopened, but all evangelistic endeavors are a percentage effort. We have never fooled ourselves into thinking one hundred percent of our effort will bring positive results. If statistics show that one out of every fifty pieces of literature handed out is read, we know that after we have distributed fifty tracks, we are on our way.

Several critical guidelines need to be observed when using any form of this method. The material should be short and attractive. People will not read what goes on and on, and they will not read what turns them off at first glance. Also, it is important to observe the established rules and laws. Housing developments and apartment complexes often have rules for such endeavors. I have known people to put their literature in mailboxes. That's against the law. Better to go through the post office and get stamps if you are going to take advantage of the mailbox.

Maybe you have some ideas about how to use this dated method. Modern printing facilities make it possible to produce great-looking literature at minimum cost.

THE CRUSADE OR EVANGELISTIC MEETING

In my lifetime, I have seen the evangelistic meeting decline from a major effort by the church to almost complete nonexistence. I've heard stories of people standing outside the building, watching and listening because there was no room on the inside. I've seen pictures of large groups of people taken to the creek for baptisms on Sunday afternoon after the revival or evangelistic meeting had closed.

Even as late as the middle years of my own ministerial labors, I had the joy of knowing what could be accomplished with an evangelistic meeting. In Indiana, we prayed and worked for months for a successful evangelistic endeavor. On Sunday morning before the meeting started that evening, we saw twenty-six people respond to the invitation to make decisions. Most of those were conversions. That number doubled before the week was over. I think more than thirty people were baptized in six days. Great results in our little town.

A few years later in Canton, Ohio, we again saw around fifty people in a five-day meeting respond for salvation in a "Lift Up Christ" crusade in our church. I often hear that the day of the evangelistic meeting or crusade is over. What I learned through my own experience is that the day of simply calling an evangelist, and perhaps a special music person, and expecting great results is over. Such an approach in our day is not likely to bring more than a handful of people out to the special meetings, despite the ability of the crusade personnel.

It is my conviction and experience that long and proper preparation with much prayer can still produce successful evangelistic meetings. But it will only happen when there are people willing to pay the price. And therein lies the reason for the latter-day failures. I once heard someone say, "You don't hold evangelistic meetings. You turn them loose." Today, they are not turned loose by oratory or a golden voice, but rather by diligent preparation and hard work. It can still be done, but only where there are willing workers to follow a well laid out plan.

DOOR-TO-DOOR VISITATION

Door-to-door visitation can take on any number of shapes. It was probably thirty-five years ago that I led a group of forty people into housing developments, apartment complexes, and mobile home parks to enroll people for our Sunday School program. As I remember, it was a program called "Action" that I borrowed from the Southern Baptist. We had moderate success. I have learned that even moderate success in evangelism is a good thing. It was a good experience for those of us who participated.

As the new preacher in one of the churches I served, I went from door-to-door in our community to introduce myself to our neighbors and offer my services. One eventual result of that effort was that a family was won to the Lord and today the husband/father has been serving as a minister for many years. In another church, after a building program, we went door-to-door with cookies, attempting to make amends for any inconvenience we might have caused them with our construction. I have probably done door-to-door visitation with a half dozen other twists. There may very well be a way for you to use this time-honored approach. We rationalize that door-to-door is out of the question today because people don't want to see us at their front doors. That has not been my experience.

HIGH ATTENDANCE DAYS

I need to point out that high attendance days are not strictly for evangelism. Rather they are for building a big one-day attendance. However, I presided over such days for years and found them to be extremely helpful to me evangelistically. As I stated in another place, the best evangelistic results come from working among those who have attended our services. The greatest evangelistic value of the high attendance day is that it provides prospects with which to work. The first time I remember promoting such a day, I think we were running about one hundred and fifty. We more than doubled that on our special day with more than three hundred fifty people present. Several people who came for the first time that Lord's day eventually were won to the Lord. Later in a church averaging around four hundred, we had more than six hundred and fifty. That day provided us with enough potential converts to keep us busy for some time.

During my years with the Town and Country Church in Shelbyville, Indiana, a high attendance day was a yearly event for us. Those days never failed to produce people with whom we would work to bring to the Lord. These days are frowned upon by many for reasons I'll not go into. But I, having a suspicious nature, suspect that the real reason this idea is frowned upon is that its success requires an abundance of planning and work. Perhaps if you are serious about reaching people for the Lord, you can find a way to make this idea work for you.

DECISION DAY

This is an idea I used only twice in my years of serving in the ministry. I think I seldom employed it because most often I was serving churches that were regularly reaching people and usually did not have a backlog of people who needed to accept the Lord. One of those two decision days did provide me with perhaps the most enthralling moment in all my years of serving the Lord. We had gone to a counseling system at decision time. As people responded, trained spiritual counselors would go with them to rooms beside and behind the platform to discuss their decisions. Afterwards, we would bring them out and introduce them to the congregation to acknowledge those decisions.

I don't remember how many people came to make decisions that Lord's day, but it was a large number. I went to the back as items were being handled by others in the worship auditorium. Looking around, I was spellbound. There were people everywhere I looked with their Bibles open talking with other people about the Lord. A couple were bowing as they prayed together. They were not only at the tables provided, but some were in the floor. I'll never forget that moment. Tears flowed as I thought, *this is the way it is supposed to be.* I think maybe that moment was the high point of my ministry.

Be warned! One does not just announce and then have decision day. There are classes to be taught, a series of letters to be composed and sent, visits to make as well as other steps to take. I know of no short cuts that take the work from any method designed for evangelism.

FAIRS, FESTIVALS ETC.

One of the churches I served went to the fair. We put our best singer on a platform and turned up the volume. Hundreds of pieces of literature were distributed to passing fair visitors. And many people went into the mobile unit where we showed a movie about conversion after which we talked with them about what they saw.

We draw thousands of people to the little town where I now live with a fall festival. Our church, for about three years set up a booth from which we distributed bottles of water with the churches name on them to visitors. If they desired, we talked with them about living water. There are numerous ways to evangelize at such events. Customize it to your church and the event and something good could happen.

STILL MORE

There are various other evangelistic ideas such as variations of the weekly church visitation program, not mentioned here because it is spoken of in other chapters. Newspaper ads, radio and TV spots, mailings of several types, prison ministry, and perhaps even a variation of the old street preacher. No, I'm not joking. We have all kinds of possibilities with the social media available to us today. Regardless of what you choose to do the job, it requires three things: work, prayer, and faith. Maybe we need to stop complaining that it won't work and find a way to get it done.

YOUR ASSIGNMENT

1. List all the outreach programs in which your church is involved.

2. List all the outreach programs in which you are directly involved.

3. Which program above could your church successfully embrace with the proper alterations?

CHAPTER 13

SCRIPTURE, QUOTATIONS, AND A FINAL WORD

I n this chapter, you will find quotations from some well-known Christians. There is also Scripture from the Old and New Testaments. The quotations, though uninspired, are for your edification and use. The Scripture is, of course, inspired of God, therefore deserving of our most diligent examination. They are passages that can be taught and preached. May it all come together to add to our convictions about getting the good news out to the world. We hope the final word will enable us to go on our way with more determination than ever to be God's heralds.

WHAT SOME GREAT CHRISTIANS SAID ABOUT EVANGELISM

"The salvation of a single soul is more important than the production or preservation of all the epics and tragedies in the world."
- C.S. Lewis

"We talk of the second coming; half the world has never heard of the first."
- Oswald J. Smith

"It is the duty of every Christian to be Christ to his neighbor."
- Martin Luther

"The Great Commission is not an option to be considered... It is a command to be obeyed."
- Hudson Taylor

"Every Christian is either a missionary or an imposter."
- Charles Spurgeon

"The Church exists for nothing else but to draw men into Christ."
- C.S. Lewis

"While women weep, as they do now, I'll fight; while children go hungry, as they do now, I'll fight; while men go to prison, in and out, as they do now, I'll fight; while there is a drunkard left, while there is a poor lost girl upon the streets, while there remains one dark soul without the light of God, I'll fight to the very end!"
- William Booth

"One of the greatest priorities of the church to-day is to mobilize the laity to do the work of evangelism."
                    - Billy Graham

"Evangelism is not a professional job for a few trained men but is instead the unrelenting responsibility of every person who belongs to the company of Jesus."
                    - Elton Trueblood

"When a man is filled with the Word of God you cannot keep him still. If a man has got the Word, he must speak or die."
                    - Dwight L. Moody

"To be a soul-winner is the happiest thing in the world."
                    - Charles Spurgeon

"All true theology has an evangelistic thrust, and all true evangelism is theology in action."
                    - J.I. Packer

"Any method of evangelism will work if God is in it."
                    - Leonard Ravenhill

"Evangelism is not salesmanship. It is not urging people, pressing them, coercing them, overwhelming them, or subduing them. Evangelism is telling a message. Evangelism is reporting good news.

- Richard Halverson

"Prayer is crucial in evangelism: Only God can change the heart of someone who is in rebellion against Him. No matter how logical our arguments or how fervent our appeals, our words will accomplish nothing unless God's Spirit prepares the way."

- Billy Graham

"Sympathy is no substitute for action."

- David Livingston

"The one who would have real success in bringing others to Christ must himself be a thoroughly converted person."

- R.A. Torrey

"Someone asked, 'Will the heathen who never heard the Gospel be saved?' It is more a question with me whether we – who have the Gospel and fail to give it to those who have not – can be saved."

- Charles Spurgeon

"In talking with a man, you want to win, talk with him in his own language."

- Henry Drummond

"All around us are people who are lost and separated from the heavenly Father, and we have a responsibility to tell them about Him."
                    - Billy Graham

"Oh, is it not a magnificent thing to be privileged thus, in any small measure, to spread the glorious tidings of our Blessed Lord?"
                    - Amy Carmichael

"We must always bear in mind that the primary purpose of our work, is not to get persons to join the church or to give up their bad habits, or to do anything else than this, to accept Jesus Christ, as their Savior."
                    - R.A Torrey

"The glory and efficiency of the gospel are staked on the men who proclaim it."
                    - E.M. Bounds

'The great majority of those who are counted believers are doing nothing towards making Christ known to their fellow men."
                    - Andrew Murray

"I never see important people – or anyone else – without having the deep realization that I am – first and foremost – an ambassador of the King of kings and Lord or lords. From the moment I enter

the room, I am thinking about how I can get the conversation around to the gospel."
                    - Billy Graham

"Because sinners are not converted by direct contact of the Holy Ghost, but by the truth, employed as a means. To expect the conversion of sinners by prayer alone, without the employment of truth, is to tempt God."
                    - Charles Finney

The law is a rough thing; Mount Sinai is a rough thing. Woe unto the watchman that warns not the ungodly."
                    - Charles Spurgeon

"Never offer men a thimbleful of Gospel."
                    - Henry Drummond

"I have never known a man who received Christ and ever regretted it."
                    - Billy Graham

"I would sooner bring one sinner to Jesus Christ than unravel all the mysteries of divine Word, for salvation is one thing we are to live for."
                    - Charles Spurgeon

SAMPLING OF OLD TESTAMENT SCRIPTURE WITH
EVANGELISTIC IMPLICATIONS

"But I have raised you up for this very purpose, that I might show you power and that my name might be proclaimed in all the earth."
Exodus 9:16

"I will proclaim the name of the Lord. Oh, praise the greatness of our God."
Deuteronomy 32:3

"Sing the praises of the Lord, enthroned in Zion; proclaim among the nations what he has done."
Psalm 9:11

"The Lord announces the word, and the women who proclaim it are a mighty throng."
Psalm 68:11

"Declare his glory among the nations, his marvelous deeds among all peoples."
Psalm 96:3

"Give praise to the Lord, proclaim his name; make known among the nations what he has done."
Psalm 105:1

"The fruit of the righteous is a tree of life; and the one who is wise saves lives."
Proverbs 11:30

"Then I heard the voice of the Lord saying, 'Whom shall I send? And who will go for us?' And I said, 'Here am I, Send me!' He

said go and tell this people: 'Be ever hearing, but never under-standing; be ever seeing, but never perceiving.'"
Isaiah 6:8-9

"In that day you will say: 'Give praise to the Lord, proclaim his name; make known among the nations what he has done, and proclaim that his name is exalted.'"
Isaiah 12:4

"You who bring good news to Zion, go up on a high mountain. You who bring good news to Jerusalem, lift up your voice with a shout, lift it up, do not be afraid; say to the towns of Judah, 'Here is your God!'"
Isaiah 40:9

"The Lord has made proclamation to the ends of the earth: "Say to Daughter Zion, 'See, your Savior comes! See, his reward is with him and his recompense accompanies him.'"
Isaiah 62:11

"But if I say, 'I will not mention his word or speak anymore in his name.' his word is in my bones. I am weary of holding it in; indeed, I cannot."
Jeremiah 20:9

"Son of man, I have made you a watchman for the people of Israel: so, hear the word I speak and give them warning from me. When I say to the wicked, 'You wicked person, you will surely die,' and you do not speak out to dissuade them from their ways, that wicked person will die for their sin, and I will hold you ac-countable for their blood. But if you do warn the wicked person to turn from their ways and they do not do so, they will die for their sin though you yourself will be saved."
Ezekiel 33:7-9

"True instruction was in his mouth and nothing false was found on his lips. He walked with me in peace and uprightness and turned many from sin."
Malachi 2:6

SELECT NEW TESTAMENT SCRIPTURE RELATED TO EVANGELISM

"From that time on Jesus began to preach, 'Repent for the kingdom of heaven has come near.'"
Matthew 4:17

"You are the salt of the earth. But if the salt loses its saltiness, how can it be made salty again? It is no longer good for anything, except to be thrown out and trampled underfoot."
Matthew 5:13

"You are the light of the world. A town built on a hill cannot be hidden."
Matthew 5:14

"Neither do people light a lamp and put it under a bowl, instead they put it on its stand, and it gives light to everyone in the house. In the same way, let your light shine before others, that they may see your good deeds and glorify your Father in heaven."
Matthew 5:15-16

"Then he said to his disciples, 'The harvest is plentiful, but the workers are few. Ask the Lord of the harvest, therefore, to send out workers into his harvest field."
Matthew 9:37-38

"Therefore, go and make disciples of all nations, baptizing them in the name of the Father and of the Son and of the Holy Spirit,

and teaching them to obey everything I have commanded you. And surely I am with you always, to the very end of the age."
Matthew 28:18, 20

"For whoever wants to save their life will lose it, but whoever loses their life for me and for the gospel will save it."
Mark 8:35

"He said to them, 'Go into all the world and preach the gospel to all creation.'"
Mark 16:15

"The Spirit of the Lord is on me, because he has anointed me to proclaim good news to the poor. He has sent me to proclaim freedom for the prisoners and recovery of sight for the blind."
Luke 4:18

"For the Son of Son of Man came to seek and to save the Lost."
Luke 19:10

"Jesus answered, 'I am the way and the truth and the life. No one comes to the Father except through me."
John 14:6

"But you will receive power when the Holy Spirit comes on you; and you will be my witnesses in Jerusalem, and in all Judea and Samaria, and to the ends of the earth."
Acts 1:8

"For this is what the Lord has commanded us; 'I have made you a light for the Gentiles, that you may bring salvation to the ends of the earth."
Acts 13:47

"For I am not ashamed of the gospel, because it is the power of God that brings salvation to everyone who believes: first to the Jews, then to the Gentiles."
Romans 1:16

"Consequently, faith comes from hearing the message, and the message is heard through the word about Christ."
Romans 10:17

"We are therefore Christ's ambassadors, as though God were making his appeal through us. We implore you on Christ's behalf; Be reconciled to God."
2 Corinthians 5:20

"To them God has chosen to make known among the Gentiles the glorious riches of this mystery, which is Christ in you, the hope of glory."
Colossians 1:27

"But you, keep your head in all situations, endure hardship, do the work of an evangelist, discharge all the duties of your ministry."
2 Timothy 4:5

"You, however, must teach what is appropriate to sound doctrine."
Titus 2:1

"But in your hearts revere Christ as Lord. Always be prepared to give an answer to everyone who asks you to give the reason for the hope that you have. But do this with gentleness and respect."
1 Peter 3:15

A FINAL WORD

According to Jesus, our mission, as Christians, is to make disciples. That process begins with evangelism. How are we doing? It's tough to measure on a wide scale. You have heard it said that you can make numbers say anything you want them to say. We may hear stats concerning church plants, new members, attendance trends, contributions etc., but not a lot about conversions. As we search for an answer, the best approach may be to simply open the eyes God gave us. What do you see happening? What do you fail to see that should be taking place? I praise God that you will observe some who have not lost sight of the mission Jesus assigned. They are diligently laboring in the field for the harvest, but they may be the exceptions. Remember, our search is not for the purpose of judging our brethren. How are *we* doing? I mean personally. That is the appropriate question to ask.

It was James who wrote, "If anyone, then, knows the good they ought to do and doesn't do it, it is sin for them" (James 4:17). We know what we ought to be doing. Are we doing it?!

Some readers may decide after consulting the latest Barna Research Group polls that the reaching of our culture demands something more than what is found here. That's okay. I would advise those people to ignore my suggestions. Go and do it your way! But don't sit around doing nothing. Don't waste time looking for an easy way. The souls of people depend on our doing something. Our Lord is counting on us. Love demands we be thoroughly involved!

"But you will receive power when the Holy Spirit comes on you; and you will be my witnesses in Jerusalem, and in all Judea and Samaria, and to the ends of the earth" (Acts 1:8).

YOUR ASSIGNMENT

1. Select your favorite quotation from those above. Why is it your favorite?

2. Which Old Testament Scripture listed above speaks loudest to you?

3. Can you find a New Testament Scripture not listed above that should be?

4. What are your plans for getting the good news out in the days ahead?